1001 Supersa

1001 Supersavers

Hints and tips to save you time and money

Pamela Donald

PIATKUS

Acknowledgements

I am most grateful to Wilma Lawson and Christine Roberts for their invaluable help and enthusiasm in preparing this collection.

First published in 1990 by
Judy Piatkus (Publishers) Limited,
5 Windmill Street, London W1P 1HF

British Library Cataloguing in Publication Data

Donald, Pamela
  1001 supersavers.
  1. Home economics
  I. Title
  640

  ISBN 0–7499–1022–4

Cover design and illustration by Ken Leeder
Designed by Sue Ryall
Illustrated by Ron McTrusty

Typeset by Phoenix Photosetting, Chatham, Kent
Printed and bound in Great Britain by
Mackays of Chatham PLC, Chatham, Kent

Contents

Introduction

The ideas in this book are well travelled and have come from amateur and expert alike.

During my time chairing the BBC Radio 4 DIY series *Homeing In*, presenting ITV's *Homework* and appearing on Daytime programmes such as BBC1's *Bazaar* and Lifestyle Channel's *Tea Break*, the response from other 'generous tippers' has been enormous, enabling me to fill many notebooks with their simple tricks for saving time and money. I thank them each and every one, from Memphis Tennessee to Kirriemuir in Scotland, these truly are the ubiquitous tips.

Pamela Donald
July 1990

Tools and Equipment

1 An old hot-water bottle with the neck cut off and stuffed with old tights and rags makes a good, free kneeling pad for low-level DIY work.

○ *Drilling and sawing . . .*

2 When drilling into a slippery surface, e.g. ceramic tiles or metal, cover the area with insulation or masking tape to avoid slipping.

3 Saws will glide better if rubbed on both sides with the stub of an old candle. Apply pressure on the downward stroke.

4 When sawing plywood, stick masking tape along the line to be cut to prevent splintering.

○ *Putty . . .*

5 To loosen stubborn putty, apply paint stripper and leave to soak for 20 minutes, or carefully heat the old putty with a hot poker, it will then come out easily.

6 Putty will keep soft and pliable for up to a year if kept completely covered in kitchen foil.

○ *Linoleum and vinyl . . .*

7 Before laying linoleum or vinyl, leave it in a heated room or in the sun all day so that the warmth penetrates the centre of the roll and makes it more pliable and less likely to crack.

8 Cut vinyl generously as it is apt to shrink. Environmentally-friendly linoleum is making a comeback – don't tack it down for a day or two to allow it to 'tread out' and prevent bulges as it is inclined to stretch.

○ *Nails and screws . . .*

9 It's impossible to hold a tin tack between thumb and forefinger, so push the tack through a piece of stiff cardboard and use this is an extension of your fingers to hold the tack in place.

10 Dip the tips of screws and nails in pure beeswax polish or petroleum jelly or press them into a bar of soap to lessen resistance, to prevent wood splitting, to stop screws rusting and to make them easier to remove should you ever need to.

11 Loosen rusted screws or nails by first putting a drop of vinegar on the heads and leaving this to soak in. If this alone doesn't do the trick the next step is to touch the head with a red hot poker, or, in the case of the screws, to insert a screwdriver into the head and tap firmly with a hammer. Or tighten the screw further to dislodge the rust before re-screwing.

12 To tighten a loose screw, remove it, glue a wooden matchstick into the hole and and screw it back in again.

13   To stop the plaster cracking when hanging a picture, place Sellotape on the desired spot before driving a nail into the wall.

14   Cut pencil stubs in suitable lengths for rawlplugs. The graphite in the pencil makes it easy for the hook or screw to enter the wood.

15   If you're nailing timber which has a tendency to split, nip off the point of the nails with a pair of pliers or pincers. This leaves a 'spade' end, which, if you position it straight across the grain, will stop the wood splintering.

Repairing, Renovating and Cleaning

16   To recondition white fridges, cookers and other kitchen appliances use bath enamel. Or stick masking tape on handles, hinges etc, put wedges of newspaper underneath, and apply car paint from a spray can in any colour you fancy.

17   Typists' white correcting fluid is good for concealing scratches on white paint, chipboard, fridges and other enamelled surfaces.

18   To remove old or unwanted laminate (Formica) cover with aluminium foil and iron over it to soften the adhesive. The laminate should then peel off.

19   Talcum powder channelled into joints or gaps silences squeaky floor boards or stair treads.

20 | Make headboards for beds from large mirrors, painted garden trellis, material over copper piping frames, bookshelves or wooden poles and rings holding a rectangular bolster.

21 | Treat mould or fungus on walls, stone floors, window frames etc, by wiping with neat household bleach before drying completely and treating with a fungicide to kill spores.

22 | Dry rot can be treated by painting with petrol until it blackens and dies. As petrol is highly flammable, take care you don't do the same!

○ *Walls . . .*

23 | To cover a crack in a wall use a piece of calico or white bandage and then paste well around the wall surface with wallpaper adhesive. Smooth the material over the hole. Once it's dry, it will tighten.

24 | The best way to remove rubble from a crack is with a pointed beer can opener. Clean out the dust with a brush.

25 | To remove splashes of cement, dirty marks or paint drips from bricks, use another brick, like an eraser, to rub it off.

26 | If you can't afford to replace ugly radiators, hide them by fixing an attractive casing of brass builders' mesh or painted garden trellis in front.

27 | Garden trellis can be painted white and attached to a not-so-perfect wall surface for a summery look, saving a plasterer's bill.

28 | When fixing trellis to an outside wall, mark where the corners will go, drill and attach cotton reels at these points and fix the trellis to this.

○ *Tiles . . .*

29 | If you're tired of your existing wall tiles, try to avoid removing them – you'll most likely damage the wall surface. Paint over them or, better still, provided that they are not cracked, just lay new tiles on top.

30 When the grouting in between tiles has become stained or discoloured, clean it using household bleach on a toothbrush.

31 You can change the colour with special grouting paint to complement or contrast with the tiles . . . It doesn't matter if you smudge it as it rubs off the tiles when dry.

○ *Baths . . .*

32 Treat stains on enamel baths by rubbing in salt with a soft cloth dampened in white spirit, vinegar or paraffin.

33 Remove corrosion around chrome taps and fittings with paraffin or damp bicarbonate of soda on a toothbrush to get into the joints.

34 To give bath sealant twice the sticking power, use a hairdryer to remove every trace of moisture around bath and washbasin surrounds before applying.

○ *Glass . . .*

35 A small chip in a glass needn't mean that it has to be thrown out. Use the finest-grained wet- and dry-glass paper and work it over the rim until it's smooth.

CHIP IN A BOTTLE

36 A large cheap slab of mirror glass becomes grand in a frame made from boards and secured to the wall with finishing nails which have no heads. Cover with silk, sackcloth or PVC etc.

37 Use bread, or damp cotton wool to pick up fragments of broken glass safely.

○ *Metals . . .*

38 Soak grease or grime from brass or copper with a hot vinegar and salt solution. Shift verdigris with neat household ammonia and salt.

39 If the metal of an object is unrecognisable when it comes your way, coat it with a paste of equal parts flour, salt and vinegar. Leave overnight and wash off the next day.

40 To save polishing and to prevent tarnish on brass doorfittings, scrub the newly-polished metal with hot water and a washing-up liquid solution. Dry with a soft cloth and apply a coat of clear acrylic metal lacquer.

41 To remove lacquer from brass, rub it with surgical spirit – don't use paint stripper.

○ *Pictures . . .*

42 To repair plaster mouldings on picture frames, use alginate, a dental impression compound obtainable from dental suppliers or your friendly neighbourhood dentist who orders it in bulk. Plastic wood putty fills cracks and holes in wooden frames.

43 Restore gilt picture frames with a mix of 1 egg white and 1 teaspoon of bicarbonate of soda. Apply with a pastry brush, leave for a few minutes then wipe off with neat washing-up liquid.

44 Make a picture frame look expensive by matching the frame to the predominant picture colour. Rubbing oil paint into un-attractive wood can add life to it.

45 A metallic paint, such as liquid leaf, applied over a primer on bare wooden frames gives a nice antique look.

46 Re-sparkle grimy picture glass with a soft cloth dipped in paraffin or methylated spirit then polish off with crumpled newspaper.

47 When re-hanging pictures and mirrors to newly-cleaned walls, first attach cornplasters at the back to stop marks reappearing.

○ *Furniture . . .*

48 Dents in stripped furniture rise again if you leave a damp cloth on them overnight and iron over it the next day.

49 Scratches in furniture will certainly improve and probably disappear if treated with cod liver oil. Leave for 24 hours before polishing off.

50 You can often fill in scratches, even tiny cracks on a wooden surface, using a child's crayon in a matching colour. Rub until it's flush with the surface. Use beeswax polish to blend it in.

51 To remove burns on furniture try rubbing with silver polish before you try anything else . . .

52 The traditional way to treat water and alcohol stains on polished surfaces is with a mixture of cigarette ash and castor oil. Treat heat stains with spirit of camphor or camphorated oil.

53 White rings also respond to a vigorous rubbing with toothpaste, or a mixture of salad oil and salt, or a dab of mayonnaise, or Brasso.

54 Cigar ash mixed with olive oil works best on white rings where furniture has been French polished. Rub light woods with a shelled brazil nut cut in half.

55 Treat white heat marks on a varnished surface, with a half and half mix of linseed oil and methylated spirits.

56 Veneer finishes react favourably to salt and olive oil mixed to a paste and left to soak in overnight. First try rubbing with the cut surface of half a shelled brazil nut.

57 Periodically rub garden furniture with linseed oil to prevent cracks and splits.

58 To stop a table leg wobbling, mix wood shavings with wood glue under it. When the glue is well set, trim away the excess.

59 To kill worms in furniture, apply paraffin to the affected parts. Use a knitting needle to poke it well into the bigger holes, and keep up the treatment daily for 10 days.

60 To recondition cheap junk shop furniture, coat it with linseed oil and leave it for at least a week to feed the wood. Add a beeswax polish shine.

61 Renovate oil or neglected leather-covered furniture with 2 parts linseed oil to 1 part white vinegar, shaken in a jar and applied with a soft cloth.

62 Secondhand cane furniture goes for a song when it becomes baggy. Sponge the whole piece with warm salt water. Turn it upside down, pour really hot water all over it and dry it in the sun. The cane will shrink and tighten.

63 For an antique wicker look, buy new but cheap wicker furniture, varnish it with several thin coats of clear varnish or use a rich brown-coloured varnish over linseed oil mixed with artists' oil paint.

○ *Hands . . .*

64 Before tackling any grubby work, rubbing petroleum jelly on your hands especially under the nails and on the wrists and forearms. Dirt will wash off easily afterwards.

65 Remove stubborn stains from hands by rubbing them over with a raw potato. Add a teaspoon of sugar to the soapy water when washing hands and all traces of grime will rinse off.

Doors
and Windows

66 If a bolt refuses to budge, a dosing from a can of Coca-Cola or a few drops of ammonia left to soak in for a couple of seconds should make it unstick.

67 Locks won't stick if powdered graphite is puffed into the mechanism. (It also stops piano pedals squeaking.) Oil attracts dirt and will eventually make the problem worse.

68 If a door is sticking, rubbing some chalk down the edge where it meets the frame and close it. When re-opened, the frame will be marked at the sticking place. Rub it down with sandpaper. Sliding doors (and drawers) will glide more easily with moist soap or candlewax rubbed along the runners.

69 Cotton reels make super door stops. Secure them to the floor with long screws and paint to blend with the decor.

70 Rub a creaking hinge with Vaseline, a lead pencil or washing-up liquid.

71 Make sash windows burglar proof – drill a hole in both outer and inner window frames and insert a sash or dual screw. Drill a second hole part of the way up the upper window and the window can be bolted even when partially open to let air in.

72 Soap sash cords on windows for easier opening.

Heating and Water Systems

73 Bleed the central heating pump of air when it has been out of use for any length of time. Run it for a couple of minutes each week throughout the summer to keep it in good working order.

74 To unclog a showerhead, undo it and poke through the holes with a pipe cleaner. Soak the perforated part in neat vinegar overnight.

75 To thaw frozen pipes and taps, apply a gentle heat from a hairdryer or place a hot-water bottle on the frozen bit. Alternatively heat firebricks in the oven and place as near the pipes as possible.

76 If the pipe is outside, bind it with rags and pour boiling water over it.

77 A few drops of glycerine added to the cistern in the lavatory provides an excellent anti-freeze.

78 A heat and light bulb which costs next to nothing to run during the night can provide just enough warmth in very cold areas to prevent freezing.

79 Add salt or anti-freeze solution to the traps of baths, sinks washbasins and WCs in extremely cold weather.

Storage

80 Shelves at eye level can be made to do double the work if you attach the lids of screw-top glass jars securely to the undersides. Fill the jars with odds and ends and screw them into the lids.

81 Small trough-like shelves on the backs of cupboard doors store fiddly things like herb jars, mustard pots, aluminium foil and clingfilm.

82 An old bicycle basket, fixed to the back of a cupboard door next to the kitchen sink, is better than a pedal bin for waste disposal.

83 Attach two empty cotton reels in a cupboard just close enough for a broom head to sit on them and its handle to hang in between.

84 To make a drawer divider, attach lengths of spare curtain track to the sides or base of the drawer as a fixing for plywood dividers.

Home Decorating

O *Painting . . .*

85 Before painting, always clean walls from the bottom upwards to avoid streaking. Add a little paraffin to the bucket of soap suds to shift the dirt quicker. Rinse well from top to bottom.

86 If you are uncertain about a new paint colour, buy test pots (available in leading brands) and paint round both sides of a corner to see how it looks in light and shade.

87 If you're only doing a short stretch of painting, it's hardly worth dirtying the roller tray. Put the tray inside a plastic bag which will mould itself to the tray when you pour the paint in. Secure the end.

88 Before painting, stand the paint tin upside down at room temperature for a few hours – it'll run better and go further. Stand enamel paint in a tin of hot water to thin it down naturally and get a porcelain-like finish.

| 89 | It is false economy to buy cheap brands of paint. They go on badly and you'll need more to get a decent cover. Buy the best makes and carefully thin down. Cheap wallpaper tears and wrinkles easily. |

| 90 | Baby food jars make ideal containers for patch-up amounts of paint or leftover wallpaper paste. |

| 91 | Paint inside the can rarely matches the colour code on the exterior. Paint the lid to show you more accurately what it looks like, and mark the level of the tin on the outside. |

| 92 | Instead of using an expensive air freshener, cut an onion in half and place in a bowl of water to draw paint smells from a room whilst you paint. Throw it away afterwards. |

| 93 | A cottonwool ear bud dipped in white shoe polish disguises the odd mark on walls before painting. |

| 94 | To stop paint dripping down your arm when painting the ceiling push the paintbrush handle through a small paper plate or an old sponge. To catch drips from the paint tin, stand it on a paper plate or kitchen foil. |

95 Tie a string across the rim of a paint or paste kettle on which to wipe off the excess paint from the brush.

96 It's a wise precaution to seal tins well inside plastic bags when buying paint. Supermarkets and DIY stores report many irate customers who complain that their car boot is ruined with spills.

97 Professional decorators always decant paint from a tin to a paint kettle for easier use. Strain the paint through a pair of old tights to remove lumps of skin. To prevent skin forming again, store tightly-sealed paint tins upside down to form a seal.

98 Prepare a new roller by soaking in soapy water for a few hours to release odd bits of fibre which slow you down by spoiling the finish. Rinse and dry the roller thoroughly before using.

99 To stop paint splashes, stick wet newspaper or clingfilm on window panes. A rim of Vaseline or washing-up liquid keeps the line from straying when painting window frames. Put kitchen foil, or plastic yoghurt cartons slit up the side, over door knobs and light fittings.

100 Loosen any pipe joints or radiator valves before painting and smear Vaseline on them. They will tighten up easily when the paint dries.

101 Stopping for a short break during painting? Wrap an emulsion brush in clingfilm or in a cloth dampened in water to stop it drying out. For oil-based paint, use white spirit on the cloth.

102 You will save up to a cupful of paint by scraping it off a roller before washing. Pop it into a small container for touch-up jobs later.

○ *Brushes . . .*

103 Before using a new brush, work the bristles back and forth in the palm of the hand to dislodge fibres or loose hairs.

104 Condition new paintbrushes by soaking in linseed oil to give them a protective coat. Clean out the oil with white spirit before you start. A blob of hair conditioner added to the last rinse before storing keeps brushes supple in between jobs.

105 Soaking paintbrushes – clip a clothes peg to the handle so the bristles don't rest on the bottom of the jar and bend.

106 For a really thorough clean, suspend brushes in paraffin (cheaper than brand cleaners). The residue falls to the bottom of the jar leaving clear liquid on top which can be poured off and used again.

107 To hang up brushes for storage, attach ring pulls from drinks cans to brush handles. Otherwise wrap in several layers of newspaper or kitchen foil to protect bristles.

108 Old brushes which have gone slightly hard will soften if the bristle part is boiled in vinegar – you'll need a cellulose thinner for solid ones.

○ *Wallpapering . . .*

109 To remove stubborn patches of old emulsion paint, paint over it with cellulose wallpaper paste and leave for 10 minutes, then remove it.

110 Don't buy expensive wallpaper strippers. Damp the walls with a warm water and washing-up liquid solution. If there are several rooms where the paper has to be removed, hire a steam stripper for the day.

111 Grease spots on wallpaper can often be removed by placing a piece of blotting paper on top of the stain and ironing over it.

112 Paste the wall not the paper when working behind radiators and guide the paper down with a padded coathanger or long-handled roller.

113 If picture pins and screws on walls are to be used again, insert matchsticks in the walls where they've been. The matches will pop through the damp wallpaper, marking the position.

114 Leave bubbles in wallpaper for 24 hours. If they haven't flattened themselves by then, prick them with a sharp knife, and with the aid of a cocktail stick or cotton bud stick some adhesive inside the cut and smooth it down with your fingers.

115 Lining paper is cheap and improves the look of less than perfect walls and acts as a base for paint too. Used under wallpaper it should be pasted on horizontally (known as cross lining) to avoid overlaps. Any left over from an unfinished roll makes inexpensive drawer liners.

116 If paper keeps rolling back on itself, secure a piece of elastic across the table with drawing pins and slide the paper under it.

117 If wallpaper seems stiff and unworkable let the paste soak in for between 2–15 minutes. Soak each length for the same time so the stretch will be the same.

118 Store spare rolls of wallpaper in old stockings or tights. Hang a length of the paper you are using in the back of a wardrobe or line drawers with it. It will gradually fade along with that on the walls and be perfect for patching. For an instant faded look, coat with lemon juice.

Conserving Energy

119 Bargains in insulating materials will only be found in the summer months, so it pays to plan ahead.

120 Listen to the radio, but not to one run on batteries. Even listening for only 2 hours a day is 40 times more expensive than plugging into mains electricity.

121 Kettles and even kettle jugs always seem to produce more boiling water than is required, so pour the extra into a thermos flask.

122 Instead of using a pre-soak and a hot wash for dirty clothes, programme your washing machine for a shorter cycle at a lower temperature. Turn it off at the point where the water and soap are mixed through. Leave it to soak for a few hours or overnight for the dirt to dissolve. Switch back on to complete the wash. Your clothes will be just as clean at half the cost.

123 Turn the tumbledryer off halfway through the programme and leave the clothes to continue to dry in the warm machine.

124   A freezer is most economical to run when full. Buy cut-price loaves at the end of the day at bakers and supermarkets to fill it up cheaply. Fill milk cartons and margarine tubs with water to freeze for blocks of ice for cold boxes and to keep bottles cold in summer.

125   A shower saves hot water, thereby reducing fuel bills – 4 or 5 people can shower in the same amount of water that 1 needs for a bath.

○   *Heating . . .*

126   Help to maintain efficiency of central heating systems with a professional service at least once a year and regularly remove dust and grime from between radiator grills and heating plates with a baby's bottle brush.

127   Check that you're not overheating rooms and water. Each 1°C (2°F) change in the room thermostat setting will make a difference of between 6 and 10 per cent in your heating costs. Most people could lower by a few degrees, wear extra clothing and remain comfortable while saving money.

128   Heating thermostats kept in a draughty hallway cannot work efficiently. A rush of cold air will produce a noticeable drop in temperature. They also react to heat spots, so don't install near a record player, lamp or TV.

129 If you fit thermostatic radiator valves to every radiator in your home you can dispense with all other thermostats except the one on the boiler. Fit them as your central heating is installed or at the annual service when radiators are drained. They save heat by allowing each room to be controlled separately. Using 'free' heat from TV sets, cookers – even body heat from a group of people – can reduce fuel bills by a fifth.

130 If you're away for long periods, consider fitting a frost thermostat to the outside of the building. This activates the heating system when the temperature drops to a very low level and pipes are in danger of freezing.

131 Time clock controls are the answer to regular warm-ups, setting the boiler in action to heat water and radiators before you get up in the morning and before you come home at the end of the day.

132 You don't need a high room temperature once you're in bed. Turning in 30 minutes earlier throughout winter can show a substantial improvement in heating costs and very likely your health too. Keeping the heat on all night is a luxury which adds at least 15 per cent to your heating bill.

133 Electric storage heaters store heat at night at off-peak electricity rates. The heat is released into the room the following day and evening.

134 Use only radiator enamel to paint radiators –metallic paint reduces the heat flow.

135 Radiator foil saves up to 15 per cent of your heating bills. Taping kitchen foil to walls behind radiators and to the underside of shelves hung a few inches above them will reflect maximum heat back into the room.

136 Don't let curtains, carpets or furniture restrict the heat flow. Curtains pulled over radiators merely heat the window panes.

137 Blinds often work better than curtains to prevent heat loss, especially where a radiator is situated under a windowsill.

| 138 | Oil for central heating tends to fluctuate in price, and usually falls in summer when demand is less. Check the costs of 3 suppliers before placing your order. |

| 139 | To make coal go further, dissolve a good handful of common washing soda in a bucket of warm water and throw it over a hundredweight of coal when delivered. |

○ *Loft insulation . . .*

| 140 | Because hot air rises, you can save up to 15 per cent of heat loss by merely unrolling 2 inches (5cm) of fibreglass insulating blanket in your loft, or packing with up to 4 inches (10cm) of the loose-fill variety. In terms of saving fuel, the material will pay for itself in 2 years. |

| 141 | A house with a sloping roof and an attic, needs insulating material fitted to the underside of the roof slope. Secure it with wire, or plastic trellis from garden centres. |

| 142 | Buy building paper to lay under blanket or loose-fill insulating material. This will get into nooks and crannies where the blanket type is more difficult to fit, and will stop loose-fill escaping. |

| 143 | Fit an excluder round the edges of the loft hatch and fix a piece of fibreglass roll on top of the trap door. |

○ *Tanks and pipes . . .*

| 144 | Buy 1 jacket, or even 2, when the sales are on, for your hot water tank, and tape or tie it on well. You'll soon recover the jacket's cost by keeping hot water at the required temperature. Even a double layer of corrugated cardboard does the job if funds are low. |

| 145 | Insulate all hot pipes leading from the hot water cylinder to taps – most cost-effective and often neglected. |

|146| Check that any hot water pipes below floorboards are adequately lagged.

|147| Make a fitted jacket for the cold tank from off-cuts of insulating blanket or buy pre-cut packs of 1 inch (2.5cm) sheet insulation. Secure with wire, string or tape. Remember to leave a gap underneath the tank, without insulating this space, to allow heat to rise to just that part from below.

|148| Buy bandage-type insulator for pipes, and secure with ties or tapes at intervals, or use the split-tube kind which you simply clip on or tape at joists or bends . . . The latter is excellent for pipes which are hard to get to. All you do is shunt it into place.

|149| Store off-cuts of fibreglass roll in a dustbin liner for patching up or filling odd corners later.

o *Ceilings and walls . . .*

|150| Polystyrene thermal foam ceiling tiles cover up cracks, stop heat escaping upwards, and, as a bonus, reduce condensation and cut down noise from above. Fireproof ceiling tiles are available at little extra cost.

|151| Sheets of polystyrene on walls and ceilings will not only keep heat in, but when coated with anti-condensation paint under emulsion or wallpaper, will cut down moisture problems too.

|152| Gaps between sinks and walls, tiles and baths etc, should be sealed with flexible waterproof sealant.

|153| Block off little or never used fireplaces. Fit and paint a plasterboard or plywood panel. Build in a ventilator to prevent damp, or have the chimney capped.

|154| Coving, the carved moulding which fits between ceiling and wall, can be bought in sections from DIY shops and will fill any gaps.

|155| Block awkward shaped holes around pipes, wires and cables with foamed polyurethane in aerosol cans.

156   Using dress or curtain material on walls instead of paint or wallpaper can work out cheaper with fewer draughts and a cosier look. First put up wooden battens and attach the cloth with a staple gun. Add a dacron padding for even more warmth and less noise . . .

○   *Windows and double glazing . . .*

157   Double glazing, installed by a reputable firm, can reduce heat loss by as much as 50 per cent. With DIY double glazing, a plastic channel is fitted, into which a pane of glass slides and is secured with special clips attached to the window panes.

158   For badly-fitting windows, use a silicone-based sealant which comes in a plastic bottle with a nozzle. Open the window and squeeze a layer around the inner frame. Close the window to press it in well and evenly cover the gaps. Open the window again to allow it to dry.

159   Sheet polythene doubles as a safety measure and elementary double glaze. Clingfilm is a lot cheaper than proprietary window insulation packs, which keep heat in and draughts out and can be applied in minutes with scissors and hairdryer.

160   Snug-fitting, closely-woven curtains, drawn at night, help keep in the heat. Detachable linings convert summer drapes to winter weight.

161   Block draughts around window frames (caused by shrinking timber), by filling the gaps with non-setting mastic compound.

○   *Floors and floorboards . . .*

162   Hardboard fixed to floorboards eliminates draughts and is usually necessary before laying sheet vinyl or tiles.

163   Narrow gaps between floorboards can be quickly sealed with strips of draught excluder. Fill larger ones with papier mâché.

164 Block off gaps between skirting and floorboards with an acrylic emulsion-type sealant or with timber beading secured to the floor with pins.

165 Invest in a felt underlay when laying carpets to seal off cold underfloor air. Building paper or even newspapers are the pauper's alternative.

166 Cork tiles are warmer than vinyl, cheaper and just as durable. Easy to lay, untreated cork can be sealed for easy cleaning.

167 For a cheap gap-stopper, where plasterboard doesn't quite fit, walls have shrunk away from beams, etc, get a packet of wallpaper paste, mix it to the consistency of thick porridge, soak strips of brown paper in it and build it up layer by layer.

○ *Avoiding draughts . . .*

168 Fit a device of brush pile 'teeth' over the inside of a letterbox opening, to fall snugly round half-posted objects. Or buy a weighted or spring-loaded flap.

169   If underdoor draughts are the problem, there are bristle strips, felt-strip underseals and two part devices for threshold and door bottom to keep out wind and rain.

170   Make a wind-stopping snake from a stocking filled with old tights, rags or kapok and decorate with material remnants, old buttons, bows etc.

171   Cover a working keyhole by fitting a brass escutcheon plate, or block an unused one with plasticine and cut out a cardboard cover to pin over it, which you can then decorate as you like.

172   Altering the structure of your home to include draught lobbies inside front or back doors, or building a porch outside, will not only trap expensive heat but most likely add to the value of your property.

Cleaning and Polishing

<hr>

173 The quickest way to spring clean a clothes line is to wind it round a long board, to stop it becoming tangled, and scrub it with a brush and hot soapy water.

174 Clean and condition coconut fibre doormats, after beating them face down outdoors, with hot water and washing soda applied with a stiff brush. When clean, dip the brush in a salt and water rinse to keep the fibre stiff.

175 Ten uses for denture tablets:

To clean slimy flower vases
Freshen dishcloths and face flannels
Sparkle costume jewellery – not pearls or precious stones
Destain tea or coffee pots if left overnight to soak – rinse well
Clean and freshen the inside of a vacuum flask

<hr>

Whiten net curtains – soak in handwarm water

Destain enamel pots and casseroles, plastic and china cups – add 2 tablets to very hot water and leave to stand for 5–10 minutes

Dissolve grease on combs and hairbrushes – add half a tablet to the wash

Clean residue inside wine carafes

Clean false teeth.

176   To clean oil paintings, grate a potato and squeeze the juice into a saucer. Apply with a soft cloth in a circular movement, or cut an onion in half and rub over the surface.

177   Papier mâché can be wiped occasionally with a cloth wrung out in warm water and a few drops of olive oil added to keep it clean. For a high polish use a good wax polish rubbed up with a soft cloth.

178   Baskets will become sturdier and last longer with an occasional wash in soap suds.

179   A teaspoon of ammonia added to the water in which blankets and flannels are washed will keep them white and prevent shrinking; keep them soft with a teaspoon of glycerine in the final rinsing water.

180   To clean modern tapestry, work Fuller's Earth or French chalk in with the fingertips or a clean cloth. Leave overnight before brushing out.

181   Sponges come up sea-fresh if soaked in a solution of 1 tablespoon of vinegar to 1 pint of water. After an hour or so all slimy traces should be removed, rinse in lightly salted water.

182   Neat household bleach on a cotton bud will clean the dirtiest teapot spout, but needs careful rinsing afterwards . . .

183   Artificial flowers can be quickly freshened by shaking them gently in the steam from a fast boiling kettle. Spraying with hair lacquer brings out the colour.

184 Recycle paper towels. After using them to dry your hands, store them in a clean milk carton under the sink. They can be used again for mopping spills, removing grease from the frying pan etc.

185 Pour any leftover Coca-Cola down the loo to bring a sparkle to the bowl.

186 Whiting applied on a chamois is used by antique dealers to polish marble.

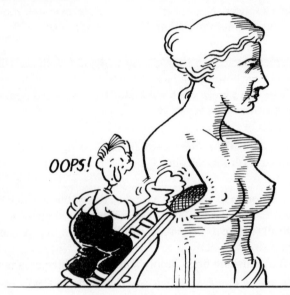

187 Clean onyx by wiping with methylated spirit.

188 Pour boiling water on used tea leaves and leave for an hour, then the liquid can be used to clean mirrors, windows, glasses, varnished doors and floors, furniture, linoleum and vinyl.

O *Mops, brushes and chamois leathers . . .*

189 Tie a knot at the end of each mop string for a much longer life. With a new broom, dip it in hot salt-water solution to toughen the bristles.

| 190 | Never throw away old toothbrushes, ideal for rubbing on cleaning agents round faucets in the bathroom or kitchen and knobs and handles on the stove. |

| 191 | Wash bristle hair and shaving brushes with ammonia. |

| 192 | Clean a chamois by dissolving 1 teaspoon of washing soda in a bowl of warm water and leaving it to soak for an hour. Wash through in the soapy water, rinse well and condition with a drop of glycerine in the final rinsing water. |

O *Metals . . .*

| 193 | Clean rusty steel with an onion cut in half. Rub well into the stains and leave the juice on for a couple of days before polishing with turpentine and washing off. |

| 194 | For very dirty brass, give it a good rub over first with a strong ammonia solution. |

| 195 | Lemon juice mixed with Brasso not only makes brass brighter but delays the tarnishing process. |

| 196 | After polishing brass, apply a little furnishing cream or olive oil and finish off with a soft cloth – especially good for bedsteads and fenders. |

| 197 | HP Sauce is a useful stand-by brass cleaner. |

| 198 | An old wives' method for a brass dip was to save your haricot bean water and pop dirty brass hooks, knobs and other fiddly bits into it. |

| 199 | Tissue paper is an instant polisher for brass, glass or crystal. |

| 200 | Clean dingy steel sinks by scouring out with a little turpentine on a piece of towelling, sluicing out with clean water and polishing with a soft rag. |

| 201 | Pewter isn't meant to shine like silver and so silver polish is unsuitable. Wash it regularly with soap and water and polish with a cabbage leaf. |

| 202 | To keep copper kettles bright, fill with hot water and polish the outside with a rag dipped in buttermilk, if you can get it. Use sour milk if you can't or salt and vinegar failing either. Filling copper kettles with boiling water before cleaning speeds the polishing process considerably. |

| 203 | Soiled copperware responds to a rub over with a cut lemon or lime and salt. Leave the juice to work for a few hours before rubbing it off with a soft cloth. Repolish with furniture polish of the non-silicone variety. |

| 204 | Paraffin will remove mildew marks from silver unless it has eaten into the metal, or try a cut lemon for unidentifiable marks. |

| 205 | For cheap and effective silver polish, use damp baking soda on a cloth. In an emergency silver can be cleaned with toothpaste. |

| 206 | A piece of chalk kept in a drawer with silver knives and forks absorbs moisture and slows down the tarnishing process. |

| 207 | Don't wear rubber gloves when polishing silver, it produces dark smears. |

| 208 | Don't store silver plate in newspaper, the printer's ink removes the plate. |

| 209 | To polish a job lot of silver, line a plastic washing-up bowl with kitchen foil. Arrange the silver in it, adding a solution of 3 tablespoons washing-up liquid to 2 pints (1.1 litres) of boiling water. Don't remove the silver until the water has stopped bubbling, at which point take it out, rinse it and dry it thoroughly. |

| 210 | Chrome cleaners are cheap and easy. Choose from paraffin on a soft cloth, or washing soda diluted in water, or dry baking soda. |

|211| A thin coat of petroleum jelly stops chrome rusting.

○ *Cutlery . . .*

|212| To store knives, rub the blades with petroleum jelly and roll in brown paper to prevent rust.

|213| To get spoons and forks sparkling clean stand them for a few minutes in a jug of soapy water with a little ammonia added.

○ *Dustbins . . .*

|214| To sanitise metal dustbins, burn a couple of newspapers or a couple of handfuls of straw in them. This absorbs grease, dirt and unpleasant smells.

|215| Plastic or rubber dustbins can be scrubbed out with a washing soda solution and a long-handled brush. Rinse well, and when dry deodorise with a sprinkling of bicarbonate of soda.

○ *Floors and furniture . . .*

|216| Frugal floor polish can be made by mixing melted candle stubs with turpentine. A more refined recipe for a quantity – melt 2 household wax candles (or the equivalent in stubs) and ½ lb (225g) of leftover bits of soap in ¼ pint (150 ml) of boiling water, and mix thoroughly. When cool, add a ¼ cup of turpentine and a ¼ cup of linseed oil. Give the mix a good stir and decant into a screw-top jar. Shake well before use.

|217| To clean linoleum and vinyl, add a little paraffin to the water to take out dirt, and grease, and polish at the same time.

|218| Beeswax comes in two varieties: bleached and yellow. Bleached beeswax is for light wood. Make a large enough quantity for floors and furniture. Grate 14 oz (400g) of yellow beeswax, add 32 fl oz (1 litre) of turpentine and leave the jar overnight. Next day shake the contents thoroughly and stand the jar in a bowl of hot water and stir until it forms a paste.

219 To make a good furniture restorer, bottle equal parts of turpentine, methylated spirits, vinegar and paraffin. When shaken well this mix is ready for use. Rub well in with a cloth, then polish off with a soft duster.

220 Condition leather upholstery with an occasional coat of wax polish. Surgical spirit sponged on leather upholstery removes grease stains.

221 A squirt of shaving foam from an aerosol is the best emergency upholstery cleaner.

222 Keep velvet-covered furniture dust-free by wiping with a chamois leather dipped in cold water and wrung out hard.

223 Squeeze old tea leaves almost dry and toss into a jar with a little kitchen salt. Sprinkle this mixture on dusty rugs and carpets and when clearing out dusty rooms – it attracts the dust and keeps the atmosphere clean.

○ *Fresheners . . .*

224 All sorts of air-fresheners cost little or nothing. Keep a box of matches to hand in the loo (out of reach of children) and light one above the lavatory after it's been flushed to remove unpleasant lingering smells.

225 Pop a pad of cotton wool soaked in cologne or aromatic oil into the bag of your vacuum cleaner for a delightful carpet freshener.

226 Crumble half a bath-cube into the final rinse of hand or machine washing to scent clothes, sheets and towels.

227 The other half of a bath-cube can be crumbled in boiling water in a bowl or jug. Stand in a bedroom for an expensive-smelling and healthy air freshener.

Soaps and
Detergents

228 Extend the life of bars of soap by taking them out of the wrapper when you buy them and placing them in drawers or in the airing cupboard, where they'll scent your belongings as they harden and therefore last longer.

229 Press a piece of kitchen foil on the underside of moist soap. The bar will last longer and be less messy.

230 Use an old washing-up bottle with the top cut off for keeping end-bits of soap. Add a drop of boiling water with each one and an occasional teaspoon of glycerine as it fills up. Stir it regularly, peel of the plastic and slice it into bars.

231 You rarely need a whole soap-filled scouring pad. Cutting them in half saves waste. Once used, wrap them in tinfoil to stop rusting.

232 When the soap from cleaning pads has gone, they are still handy as steel wool. Keep them in a screw-top jar with water and a dash of washing-up liquid to prevent rust and slime.

233 Your washing-up liquid will go twice as far if you always buy the top-quality brands and decant half the amount into an empty container. Top them both up with water.

234 Make useful funnels by cutting the tops off plastic bottles of washing-up liquid.

235 Vinegar in washing-up water removes grease, sparkles china and kills bacteria.

Irons
and Kettles

236 Cure a sticky or scratched iron by wrapping a piece of soap in a handkerchief and rubbing this over the face of the iron a few times while it's still hot.

237 Unclog a steam iron with a drink of vinegar. Leave the vinegar to sit in a warm iron until the sediment dissolves. Drain and refill the iron and it's ready for use.

238 Rainwater keeps irons clog-free.

239 A brick makes a better rest for an iron than a metal stand which draws the heat out quickly.

240 Prevent kettles from furring by putting a few glass marbles or a clean oyster shell in the bottom to stop a build up of scale.

241 | De-scale a kettle by half filling it with a solution of equal parts vinegar and water. (Do not completely fill as vinegar will expand.) Boil for a couple of minutes then leave liquid to cool while the scale dissolves. Rinse thoroughly.

242 | Don't leave water in a jug kettle overnight – swill it out and stand it upside down on a tea-towel to cut down the build up of scale.

Pots and Pans

243 | Aluminium saucepans which become discoloured can be cleaned by boiling fruit peelings such as apple skins in them until marks disappear. Or three quarters fill the pan with a weak water and vinegar solution, bring it slowly to the boil and simmer for 5 minutes. Rinse well with cold water.

244 | Never use washing soda on aluminium – rub stubborn stains with sand or salt on a damp cloth until they've gone.

245 | Burnt saucepans other than aluminium can be cleaned with cold water containing a handful of washing soda or detergent. Leave it to stand for a couple of hours or preferably overnight. Boil up and after a few minutes the burnt remains should loosen quite easily.

246 | If an aluminium pot is burnt add a small onion and some water to the pot. As it boils up, all the burnt matter will rise with it.

247 | Always add hot water to hot pans when soaking to avoid damaging the surface.

248 | Never use hot water to clean anything which cooks or sticks when heated e.g. use only cold or lukewarm water to clean raw egg utensils or milk pans. Wash floured baking boards under a cold tap before washing in soapy water.

Curtains

249 Mouldy shower curtains will look like new after a soaking in ½ a cupful of bleach and a ¼ cup of detergent. Soak for 20 minutes, rinse and drip dry.

250 Put dirty curtain rings and runners into a bowl containing hot water and vinegar – 2 parts vinegar to 1 of water – and let them soak for a few hours before rubbing with a rough towel.

251 When rehanging washed or dry-cleaned curtains, change them round so that the previous outer edges now hang on the inside where they catch the light. This way they'll fade evenly.

O *Blinds . . .*

252 To clean blinds of the slatted variety, use either an L-shaped crust of bread, or wear an old pair of fabric gloves and immerse your hands in soapy water. Pop woolly socks on your hands – ideal for a quick dry-clean.

253 To clean linen blinds, keep them on their rollers and place them on the side of the bath for a gentle wash in tepid water and washing-up liquid.

Carpets

254 For carpets where the treads are showing, try a strong solution of a dye matching the most prominent colour. Apply to the worn parts with a toothbrush and dry thoroughly.

255 For small worn areas or scorch marks, colour the treads with felt tip pens in corresponding colours. Remove charred fibres with sandpaper.

256 | Dents in carpets will come out if an ice cube is left to melt on the spot overnight. Next day, iron over a cloth until bone dry.

257 | To remove wax, oil or grease from a carpet, iron through blotting paper and rub off with turpentine on a clean rag.

258 | Treat burns on a carpet immediately, by rubbing over affected area with a slice of raw potato.

259 | Carpet cleaners which are safe and effective are oatmeal, cornflour, baking soda and salt. Sprinkle on, rub in and vacuum off after 2 hours.

260 | Ink and soot spills on carpets should be covered immediately with a generous pile of salt. Remove the surface with knife or teaspoon, repeat until the stain is absorbed, then rub over with a cut lemon.

261 | Carpets should always be brushed or hoovered in the direction of the pile otherwise you'll brush the dust in rather than out.

262 | To remove dog hairs efficiently after sweeping or hoovering, do an occasional hands and knees job with a damp rubber window blade.

263 | Make your own carpet shampoo by shredding ½ oz (12.5g) of soap into ½ pint (300ml) of boiling water to which is added a teaspoon of ammonia and a small lump of washing soda. Dip a scrubbing-brush into this and rub the carpet a section at a time. Rinse with a clean cloth constantly wrung out in a mild water and vinegar solution. Dry with clean towelling rags.

264 | To stop dust rising, dip the tips of the bristles of a stiff carpet-brush in water at intervals when hand brushing rugs and stair carpets.

265 | For faded carpets, make up a solution of 1 pint (600 ml) vinegar to 3 pints (1.7 litres) boiling water, rub on with a well-wrung cloth to greatly enhance the colour.

266 | After a carpet has been shampooed, put wedges of white tissue under furniture where it might leave dents or rust spots.

267 | Damp rubber gloves will remove fluff and hairs from carpets and upholstery in an instant.

268 | Carpets, rugs and garments where the colours are likely to bleed can be safely washed with potato water. Grate 2 potatoes and add to a pint of water in a basin. Let it soak for a while, stirring regularly. Strain the potato liquid through a sieve into another pint of water. Once this has settled pour the clear part into a bottle and apply it carefully with a sponge. Rinse off with cold water.

○ *Rugs . . .*

269 | To clean oriental rugs, lie them face-down in the snow or on damp grass for a couple of hours and then walk on them. Then beat them over a clothes line.

270 | Rugs won't slip on polished floors if rubber jam jar rings are sewn on the corner and at the centre. Alternatively, glue on strips cut from an old hot-water bottle or bicycle inner tube . . .

271 | If the corners of rugs start to curl, sew a triangular pocket containing a lead weight (obtainable from hardware shops) at each corner.

Windows, Mirrors and Glass

272 | To clean a glass decanter, break eggshells into tiny pieces and place inside with a pinch of bicarbonate of soda. Fill up with warm water, shake and leave to work overnight. Next day shake out with warm soapy water, rinse with plain water. Or fill with a solution of vinegar and salt, leave to soak for an hour, shake, tip out the solution, wash and rinse.

273 | For decanters which smell, pop a teaspoon of powdered mustard into them, top up with water, shake and leave to sit a while before rinsing.

274   If a stopper sticks in a decanter, tap around it gently with another glass stopper. This method of tapping like with like also works successfully on flower pots, stacked cups etc.

275   Alternatively, grip the stopper with a rubber glove or secure a rubber band round it for a better grip.

276   When glasses stick inside each other, pour neat washing-up liquid all around the rim and soak in warm water.

277   Steamy windows or mirrors in kitchens or bathrooms need a quick polish with a glycerine rag, or a drop of bath oil rubbed on the glass.

278   To clean paintwork on windows, dip a piece of old flannel or a woolly sock in some paraffin to remove the dirt. Remove with a clean soft cloth. The oily rags make good firelighters later.

279   When cleaning windows, dry one side of the pane horizontally, the other side with vertical strokes. This makes it easier to locate stubborn smears.

280   Wash windows with newspapers crumpled up and thrown into a bowl of tepid water with ammonia, methylated spirits or vinegar – use 3 tablespoons ammonia to 4 pints (2.3 litres) of water. Polish with dry newspaper.

Everyday Objects

281 Leave messages for the milkman and others who call in a waterproof plastic bag secured with a clothes peg or rubber band.

282 Don't buy pedal bin liners when you can get an ample supply of free plastic carrier bags from supermarkets etc. Use the handles as ties when they're full up.

283 To prevent a squeezy sponge mop from drying out and cracking, wash it in cold salt water and pop a plastic bag over it.

284 If you have long nails, turn new rubber gloves inside out and put plasters across the tips for extra protection.

285 A dash of talcum powder inside new household gloves stops the rubber perishing and keeps your hands from becoming hot and clammy.

286 Rubber gloves which are merely punctured can go on to serve as gardening gloves.

287 Buy colourful PVC cloth at sale time to make practical and pretty tablecloths for the kitchen and picnics or line a linen basket with a remnant. Easy to wipe clean and ideal for wet towels, and no jagged edges to snag your clothes.

288 For a make-shift sink tidy, an ordinary flower pot takes waste pieces, and has a useful drainage hole at the bottom.

289 Prevent mustiness in a plated or silver teapot by placing a lump of sugar inside when it's completely dry. It will keep it moisture-free and also prevent rust.

290 Cellars which have become damp as well as cold will dry out if 2 lbs (900g) of kitchen salt is divided into 4 equal parts and placed in tins in each corner of the cellar. When saturated, the tins of salt can be dried out by standing them on a warm stove, making the salt re-usable.

291 Put a folded newspaper under the door mat to gather up dust and dirt.

292 It wasn't just for tidiness that servants ironed newspapers, the newsprint won't come off on your hands afterwards.

293 Reading a newspaper out of doors is less of a battle if a paperclip is inserted into the centrefold to stop the pages coming apart.

294 Attach a paperclip or a small button at the end of a roll of Sellotape to find the end easily and save fiddling time.

295 A roll of Sellotape that appears to be gummed solid will loosen if held over steam for a few seconds.

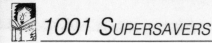

296   If sheets are folded in four before they're put in the washing machine then pegged on the line in the same folds, you can get away without ironing them.

297   When hanging out clothes, hang a loop of tape or string around your neck and clip the pegs on this to keep them handy.

298   Versatile clothes pegs close cereal packets and polythene bags containing fridge and freezer food, keep bills tidy, file petrol receipts in the car, and, when clipped to the edges of the tables, stop tablecloths flying around at barbecues.

299   Stretch plastic-coated curtain wire across the back of the airing cupboard door for hanging underwear and socks and things.

300   An old sponge, or a piece of foam rubber, cut to fit the base of an umbrella stand will gather drips.

301   After defrosting a fridge or freezer, wipe round the inside with glycerine on a rag. This will speed up the defrosting process next time.

302   Strengthen unglazed earthenware by rubbing with a cut onion or garlic clove on its outside surface.

303   Sharpen your kitchen scissors by trying to cut the neck off a milk bottle. Or cut sandpaper with them.

304   If you have difficulty opening a screw-top jar or bottle, try running it under a hot tap for a few seconds before trying again, or grip it with sandpaper.

305   Sherry bottle tops are useful standbys for recorking other bottles, such as wine bottles, if the original cork was broken during its removal.

306   A cork can be made to refit a bottle if you first soak it in boiling water to make it pliable.

Books

307   Place pieces of charcoal in the space between books and walls which might be damp, to prevent mildew . . .

308   As damp is the biggest enemy of books, never pack them so tightly that the air can't circulate around them.

309   Torn books can often be mended by using the white of an egg on a pastry brush to glue the edges together.

310   If leather book covers which are spotted with mould are rubbed with oil of lavender, they will not only be cleaned but protected from mould in future.

311   To treat leather book bindings, equal parts of milk and egg white beaten together will clean and revive them. Rub on gently with a soft flannel and polish with an old silk handkerchief.

Fires and Fireplaces

312   Keep old newspapers, travel brochures, magazines etc, to recycle as fuel bricks for the fire. Soak them in water until they become pulp. Tear them up and squeeze hard into balls. Leave in a warm place to dry.

313   Chimney flue cleaners are expensive. Make your own by mixing 1 lb (450g) of flowers of sulphur and ½ lb (225g) of powdered salt petre. Occasionally when the fire is burning bright and clear, throw a handful of this mixture on the flames to remove much of the accumulated soot.

314 Chimney fires will be quickly extinguished by throwing a good quantity of kitchen salt on the flames. Or douse the fire with lots of water and the steam which rises will gradually put out the flames in the chimney.

315 Potato peelings burnt on the fire not only help it to burn more evenly but stop soot forming in the chimney.

316 Milk cartons and orange peel (dried) can be used up as free fire lighters.

317 To make a fire last, fill a dampened cardboard egg carton with chips and dust from the coal bunker, put this in the centre of the fire and it should burn evenly and slowly for many hours.

318 Clean a discoloured gas fire, stained with smoke, by sprinkling liberally with salt when cold. Light the gas to burn the salt away and at the same time leave the fire clean.

Repairs and Renovations

319 To glue broken china, first grease round its edges to prevent stray glue setting as it oozes from the joint. Wipe with a damp cloth.

320   An old clock which appears to have stopped for the last time will often get going again if placed in a barely warm oven – about meringue temperature.

321   Facial scratches on clocks and watches will be improved by rubbing with Brasso.

322   When a sheet or blanket becomes worn in the centre, cut it in half (through the thin part down the middle) and reverse the halves, putting the middle to the outside and the outside to the middle. The centre seam can be quickly run up and the sides hemstitched.

323   Recycle worn bath towels – cut up into hand towels and face flannels first, cleaning rags later.

324   Turn old sheets and tablecloths into cot sheets, napkins etc.

325   It's expensive to have old quilts and eiderdowns converted professionally to modern duvets. Give them new life and usefulness by fixing velcro strips or studs at the corners and at the corresponding corners inside a single duvet cover.

Stain Removal

326   Keep a box of dry-cleaning substitutes including amyl acetate, phials of lighter fuel, Fuller's Earth (gentle on delicates) and glycerine (which loosens stubborn stains on material which can then be washed or treated with other cleaning agents).

327   The oldest and often best method of taking stains out of white napkins, sheets, table linens etc, was to wash them and boil them and then spread them in the hot sun for a safe and natural bleach.

328   To remove tea or blood stains from blankets, cover a deep bowl with the stained parts. Sprinkle thinly with borax and pour lukewarm water through the blanket.

329 Ink stains on bed linen will often succumb to a good rub with a slice of juicy lemon or a ripe tomato cut in half. Wash in the usual way afterwards.

330 Olive, cod-liver and assorted nut and vegetable oils are best treated with carbon tetrachloride. Drape the soiled article over a small bowl and stretch a stout elastic band round the rim, to hold the material in place. Rub well in with a small sponge and if washable, immerse the garment in soap suds afterwards and rinse well.

331 Machine oil stains can be covered with lard, washed with cold water and then with hot soapy water, or rub with petrol on a clean cloth.

332 Tar marks – soak a piece of white rag in eucalyptus oil and rub it on the affected part until the area is quite clean. Suitable for delicate materials.

333 Grass – wet with cold water, cover with cream of tartar and, if possible put in the sun to bleach.

334 With unidentifiable grease stains on light material make a paste with Fuller's Earth and cold water and cover the mark with it. Allow it to dry, then brush off. Safe for use with non-fast colours.

335 Stained eiderdowns, quilts or duvets. Soak the quilt for 10 minutes in a good lather of Woolite, or similar hand-wash solution to which you've added a tablespoon of household ammonia. Then squeeze it out and agitate it in the water for a bit longer. If it's still dirty, rinse the suds out in clear water and repeat the process. Squeeze out any surplus water between bath towels after wringing by hand. Take off the line at frequent intervals and shake well.

336 Paint stains are removed with hot vinegar.

337 For biro marks, spray the marks with fly spray to dissolve the ink then wash out in mild soap and water solution and rinse.

338 A buckram lampshade and lace trimmings can be dry-cleaned with talcum powder or powdered magnesia. Leave overnight and the dust and powder can then be removed with a clean soft brush.

339 Tea, coffee and cocoa stains can be removed by sponging with warm water with a little borax added to it, before they have time to dry.

340 Stains on dralon upholstery can be sponged with a solution of 1 dessertspoon of vinegar to ½ pint (300 ml) of lukewarm water.

341 Wine stains squirted with a soda syphon won't leave a mark.

342 Red wine stains can be removed with white wine, but a pile of salt seems less wasteful.

343 Soak fabric with grease stains in a solution of Coca-Cola and plain tepid water.

344 Scorch marks should be soaked instantly in cold milk.

Chef's Tips

Meat

345 Seasoned flour left over from coating meat, chicken or liver for frying can be used later for thickening the pan juices.

346 When browning meat for stews and casseroles, pop the pieces in a polythene bag to which you've already added flour, salt and pepper, parsley or other chopped herbs for flavour. Shake the bag to mix the ingredients quickly and evenly.

347 Porridge oats or bulgar wheat will thicken and make runny mince dishes go further. Use about 2 tablespoons per lb (450g) of meat.

348 Add a tablespoon of vinegar to a curry or stew to tenderise the cheapest cuts – and add flavour too.

349 If meat or poultry has been kept for some time and is strong-smelling, wash it in cold water and vinegar to remove the smell. If the smell persists it's best to throw it away.

|350| Chicken or beef stock can be frozen in ice trays, then stored as cubes in plastic bags in the freezer.

|351| To clarify meat dripping – put the fat in a basin with just enough boiling water to cover and stir well as it softens. When it's cool the dripping will solidify and this lump of fat can be removed leaving a tasty liquid for soups or gravy beneath.

|352| Always put meat on a rack in a roasting tin. This stops the base becoming overcooked.

|353| For healthy overfried bacon, hold the slices under cold water for a few seconds, wipe off the water with kitchen towel and lay the bacon in an earthenware or enamel dish. Cook in the oven until it's as you like it – no additional fat is needed.

|354| Keep tinned meat in the fridge; it's quick and easy to slice when needed.

|355| Make supersavings if you have a freezer, by asking the butcher to cut up half a lamb or pig for you. The biggest selection of cheaper cuts is to be found in shops in poorer areas.

○ *Game . . .*

|356| To test if game is hung, pull a feather from the plumage at the lower back near the tail. The bird is considered 'high' enough to be eaten when tailfeathers come out easily.

| 357 | A quicker way to pluck game or poultry is first to plunge the bird into boiling water for about a minute. It will not only be easier to pluck, but it will stop the feathers from flying around. |

○ *Hamburgers . . .*

| 358 | Moisten your hands with water before shaping hamburgers. Water rather than flour works as a non-sticking agent. |

| 359 | Add 4 fl oz (100 ml) of water to 1 lb (450g) of meat to get an extra portion of moist hamburgers. |

| 360 | Plastic lids from coffee cans and other containers make ideal dividers when hamburgers are being prepared for the freezer. |

Fish

| 361 | One minute in hot water before cooking kippers reduces excessive oiliness without reducing the moisture content. |

| 362 | If kippers have become dry or if they are too strongly smoked, soaking them in hot water for an hour before drying off and cooking will restore their plumpness and improve the flavour. |

| 363 | Anchovy fillets and smoked salmon which have a too salty taste should be soaked in milk for about 30 minutes to reduce the saltiness. |

| 364 | To freeze fish, pop it in a clean milk carton and top up with water. |

| 365 | Skin fish quicker by dipping your wet hands in salt to get a better grip. |

| 366 | A quick and delicious way to prepare salmon is to plunge it into boiling water seasoned with a little lemon juice, salt and pepper, boil gently for 3 minutes, cover and set it aside to cool in the liquid. |

367 Banish strong fish smells from pans and cooking utensils by emptying tea leaves from the pot into the pan and half filling with water. Leave for as long as it takes to do the rest of the washing-up. Alternatively, put lemon juice and water in the pan and bring it to the boil. Pour it away and rinse well.

Vegetables

368 If you soak dried beans, peas and other legumes overnight in water to which you've added a teaspoon of bicarbonate of soda, they'll keep their colour and be much softer, cutting down cooking time. However, they'll also lose some of their vitamin C content.

369 Don't salt dried peas, beans etc until the end of the cooking process, or you'll turn them into bullets.

370 Don't throw out hard beans, peas or whatever, they will serve as excellent weights for baking pastry blind.

371 Greens won't boil over if you pop a small piece of fat into the boiling water during cooking.

372 Add lemon juice to boiling water when cooking cauliflower for a snowy white stalk without the strong smell.

373 Cut the cost of cooking a variety of vegetables, by steaming the fast-cook varieties – Brussels sprouts, courgettes, leeks etc – over slower cooking root vegetables such as potatoes, carrot and swede.

374 If vegetables have become too soggy to serve them in their whole state, mash them into a purée and dry off as much moisture as possible by heating in a pan and stirring in a knob of butter. Sprinkle with sunflower seeds before serving.

375 Sugar and butter added to geriatric carrots which are cooked in just enough lightly salted water to cover them, improves their taste greatly.

○   *Salads . . .*

376 Leftover salad – dressing and all – liquidised quickly in a blender with a pint of tomato juice and a few drops of Tabasco, becomes a delicious Mock Gazpacho. Garnish with croutons, diced green peppers or cucumber.

377 When washing lettuce, a few drops of lemon juice added to the water will not only wash out earth and slugs, but will crispen it wonderfully. Don't use salt – it makes lettuce go limp.

378 Never toss a green salad in vinaigrette dressing until absolutely the last moment before it's served. Acid from the vinegar will make the lettuce collapse.

379 Washed lettuce will last a long time if kept in a plastic container with a tightly fitting lid in the fridge.

380 A lettuce leaf dropped into a pot of homemade soup will absorb excess fat from the surface.

381 Many salad vegetables will revive if soaked for a couple of minutes in ice-cold water (add cubes), dried thoroughly and put in the fridge for a few hours wrapped loosely in a damp tea-towel.

382 To keep watercress fresh, invert it in a bowl of very cold water so that it can drink through its leaves.

| 383 | To keep celery fresh, chop the bottoms off the stalks and stand them in a jug of chilled water. |

| 384 | Make your own celery flakes. Cut and wash the leaves from celery stalks, dry them on a baking tray in a low oven, crumble them when bone dry and store in air-tight jars. |

| 385 | To ripen green tomatoes – you can pop them in brown paper bags and leave them on a sunny windowsill or wrap them in newspapers and keep them in a drawer. When a whole truss falls off a plant, hang it up near a light window in a warm kitchen and the tomatoes will gradually ripen on the stalks. |

| 386 | To peel tomatoes easily, pour boiling water over them and leave to stand in the water for a couple of minutes before peeling. The skins will slide off easily. Do this for grapes and oranges too. |

| 387 | Treat wooden salad bowls with a thin coating of olive oil on kitchen paper to clean and protect the surface. Rub it with a cut clove of garlic before the salad is added. Never wash wooden bowls if possible – clean with oil and a little salt on kitchen paper. |

○ *Potatoes . . .*

| 388 | You can prepare new potatoes well before their cooking time and stop them going brown by adding half a cupful of milk to enough cold water to cover. Stop other potatoes from going brown with a slice of bread in the water. |

| 389 | Before scraping new potatoes, leave them to soak for 5 minutes in hot water to which a generous pinch of bicarbonate of soda has been added. The skins will now come off easily. |

| 390 | For speed and tidiness, clean and peel potatoes inside a colander in a bowl of water. Then just lift the colander and peelings out. |

| 391 | Quick Bake Potatoes – before salting and popping in the oven, allow them to stand in hot water for 15 minutes, or stick small skewers through the middle to conduct the heat in half the time. |

| 392 | For light and creamy mashed potato, the milk should be heated before adding it to the potatoes with a knob of butter in the pan. |

| 393 | If potatoes have cooked ahead of the rest of the meal, mash the potatoes with butter, then pour the hot milk carefully on top. Keep the pan in a warm place and the potatoes will stay moist and heated through until required. |

| 394 | Quick crispy roast potatoes are guaranteed by first par-boiling the potatoes and rolling them in seasoned flour before adding them to the hot fat. |

| 395 | For crisper chipped potatoes, pour salted, boiling water over the uncooked chips, drain them and dry well before cooking. |

| 396 | To absorb the fat from greasy chips, either place them on paper towels and sprinkle lightly with salt as they're taken from the pan, or shake them in a large paper bag. |

O   *Onions and garlic . . .*

| 397 | Peeling onions won't be such a tear-jerking performance if you hold a fork or spoon between clenched teeth. |

| 398 | Remove the smells of onion, garlic and other strong flavours from your hands by rubbing them with a little dried mustard, cold water and salt. Or rub fresh parsley vigorously into the skin to release the juice. |

| 399 | Sprinkle a little salt on a garlic clove so that it won't stick to the knife, chopping board or garlic press when being crushed or chopped. |

| 400 | Where garlic and onion are fried in a recipe, fry the onion first until it is hot, then add the garlic which burns easily and needs less cooking time. |

| 401 | Keep half-used onions or green peppers fresh for longer by storing them dry in screw-top jars in the refrigerator. |

○ *Herbs . . .*

402 Preserve a winter supply of parsley. Hold a bunch by the stems and dip it in boiling water until it's vivid green. Put in a hot oven to dry and finally rub it between the hands or chop it and store in jars.

403 Or put bunches in bags and store in the freezer (having washed and dried it thoroughly). Before defrosting, smash the parsley up while it is still inside the bag and shake out the amount required.

404 If you have more fresh herbs than you can use at one time, freeze the surplus amount in ice cubes, to add to soups, casseroles and sauces.

Fruit

405 Fruit which is overripe, can be puréed with sugar and whipped cream, and a squeeze of lemon added, to re-emerge as a delicious fruit fool.

406 Speed the ripening of avocados by leaving them in an airing cupboard or barely warm oven overnight. Sealing them in a brown paper bag will also soften them.

407 To stop bananas and other fruit which discolours quickly from going brown as you prepare a fruit salad, sprinkle with lemon juice.

○ *Lemons . . .*

408 To keep lemons fresh, store them in a jar of cold water, changed daily.

409 To get the maximum amount of juice from a lemon warm it slightly in the oven, or pop it in boiling water or the microwave for a few seconds. Even rolling it in the warmth of your palms will noticeably increase the yield.

410 If you only want a little lemon juice, don't cut the lemon and have the rest go dry. Drop it into boiling water to heat it through, then stick a knitting needle or a fork in it and squeeze. Wrap the lemon in tin foil and keep fresh in the fridge.

411 Grating orange and lemon peel can be messy and wasteful, but not if the grater has been run under the cold water tap to make it non-stick.

412 Without a proper gadget for removing lemon zest, you can absorb the tangy flavour needed for puddings by rubbing lump sugar over the skin.

Rice, Pasta and Noodles

413 Add a teaspoon of oil to the water when cooking rice, it will be less likely to boil over.

414 A little juice or a slice from a lemon added to rice in the cooking keeps it white and grainy.

415 Quick method for perfect rice. Use double the amount of salted water to rice, bring it all to the boil and simmer with the lid on for 10 minutes. Don't stir during cooking. Remove from the heat and leave aside in a warm place for another 10 minutes. Fluff up with a fork just before serving.

416 Add uncooked grains to cooking oil in a hot pan and then follow the boiled method for quick fried rice.

417   If rice is overcooked, salvage it by adding a few sultanas, a small tin of evaporated milk and some sugar and heating it through for rice pudding.

418   Or pretend you meant it to be savoury rice by adding a tin of drained and chopped Italian tomatoes, a dash of tomato purée, some chopped black olives and a few pine kernels. Top with breadcrumbs and pop under the grill.

419   Add a generous tablespoon of oil to the salted water in which you cook pasta. It stops it sticking together during the boiling process.

420   Pasta and noodles and other starchy dishes won't boil over if you remember to rub the inside of the pan with vegetable oil first.

421   Add a couple of drops of yellow food colouring to packet noodles and you can pretend they are the fresh homemade variety.

Condiments and Sauces

422   Keep a kitchen shaker handy containing 6 parts salt to 1 part pepper so that you always have instant seasoning ready.

423   White pepper pots won't clog at the holes if you place a dried pea in with the pepper.

424   Salt pots run freely with a few grains of rice in with the salt.

425   When preparing English mustard from powder, remember that it's strong when mixed with water, but milk gives it a mild flavour and beer a spicy tang.

426   Chopping the mint and sugar together when making fresh mint sauce makes the job easier.

427	White wine left over at the end of the bottle can be added to vinegar.
428	If homemade mayonnaise separates, beat in an extra egg yolk a little at a time.
429	Sandwich fillings of meat, fish or cheese will go further if minced or grated first with a little mayonnaise.
430	If olive oil becomes solid in the bottle during cold weather, stand the bottle in a jug of warm water until it becomes liquid again.
431	If a sauce looks too greasy on top after cooking, a slice of bread on the surface will quickly mop up the surplus.
432	Soup, stews or other dishes which have been oversalted can be cured by the addition of a few slices of raw potato in the final stages of cooking.

Eggs

433	Test eggs for freshness in a bucket of cold water. If they rise to the top they are unusable; if they tip on one end, use them up pretty quickly but if they lie on their sides they're fresh. Air gets into stale eggs, making them lighter.

|434| A fresh egg should keep a firm set when broken into a frying pan, only old eggs run all over the place.

|435| When putting all your eggs in one basket, put an X on the ones to be used up first.

|436| Scrambled egg is less likely to stick to the pan if the butter is melted thoroughly and swirled round bottom and sides to coat the pan before the eggs are added.

|437| To make omelette pans non-stick, heat the pan well before using, then scour it out with salt on a wedge of greaseproof paper. Always make sure the butter is smoking hot before adding the eggs to the pan. An omelette pan must have a heavy metal bottom; it should also only be used for omelettes or pancakes.

|438| Leftover egg yolks dropped in a bowl of cold water and stored in a cool place will keep for several days.

|439| To separate an egg yolk from the white, break the egg into a saucer, place a small upturned wine glass over the yolk and pour off the white.

|440| Before beating egg whites for meringue making rub the inside of a mixing bowl with lemon to remove any traces of grease. Using a large bowl increases the chances of success further, and adding a pinch of salt and removing every scrap of yolk ensures a dry, fluffy mixture.

O *Boiled . . .*

|441| When taking eggs from the fridge, cover them with cold water to prevent them cracking as you bring them to the boil. Plunging cold eggs into boiling water is a sure way to crack them.

|442| Prick an egg with a clean pin before putting it in boiling water and it won't crack. A safety pin in the boiling water will also stop eggs cracking.

443 | Hardboiled eggs plunged into cold water as soon as they're taken off the boil won't become discoloured around the yolks.

444 | When boiled eggs are taken from the heat, a sharp tap with a spoon at the pointed end to crack the shell will stop them cooking further.

445 | When hardboiling eggs for Easter, add onion skins to produce a rich golden brown colour. Tie grasses round to form a pattern.

○ *Poached . . .*

446 | When poaching eggs bring the poaching water to the boil and turn the heat off. Swirl the water vigorously with a spoon and gently break the egg into the middle to keep it from spreading. Put the lid on for a couple of minutes and the egg will cook gently in the hot water without becoming rubbery.

447 | Poached eggs will keep their shape in cooking if a teaspoon of vinegar is added to the boiling water. It helps to break each egg into a saucer first before sliding them into the pan. Never use salt instead of vinegar or it will break up the egg white and separate it from the yolk.

Dairy Produce

448 | For a quick healthy breakfast without cooking, add 1–2 ozs (25–50g) sultanas to a small pot of yoghurt and leave overnight. This DIY fruit yoghurt can also be used in cheesecake.

○ *Milk . . .*

449 | To keep milk fresh without a fridge, decant the milk into an ordinary screw-top bottle and make a blanket cover for the bottle. Stitch it up the side to secure it, then dip the whole

thing in cold water. Hang it up in the shade out of doors or keep in a cool pantry. As long as the blanket is kept wet, the milk will stay cold.

450 Keep a tin of evaporated milk chilled in the fridge, for easy thickening with a whisk when required.

451 If milk is about to boil over the rim of the pan, quickly take it off the heat and give the bottom of the pan a sharp knock as you put it down . . .

452 Put cold water in a milk pan first, swirling it round and emptying it out before adding milk or making custard. This stops the milk sticking to the pan when heated.

453 Never throw out milk which is 'on the turn'. Scones and cakes made with soured milk are a whole lot lighter.

○ *Cream . . .*

454 Cream beats better if the bowl, whisk and cream are all thoroughly chilled.

455 Add sugar to double cream before whipping it up, rather than afterwards to lessen the risk of overbeating it.

456 Whipped double cream will go further if yoghurt or whipped egg white is folded in – and it's less fattening too.

457 To counteract too much seasoning, add some cream to the dish.

458 Recycle whipping cream by piping it or dropping it by the spoonful on to kitchen foil and freezing it. Store the pieces in freezer bags for garnishing cakes and puddings later. Alternatively, you can freeze it on kitchen foil in a cake tin to make a round and when it's set, pop it in a freezer bag. Defrost it at a later date ready to sandwich a sponge cake.

459 If cream is beginning to go off, add a pinch of baking soda. It gets rid of the sour taste and stops the curdling process.

460   If whipped cream has gone watery, try resurrecting it by folding in an egg white. Chill thoroughly and when rebeaten it will fluff up again. Or carefully stir in some single or unwhipped cream.

○ **Butter . . .**

461   Before you cream butter, rinse the bowl in boiling water; it will now cream easily.

462   To make hard butter soft for quick spreading, add a little boiling water drop by drop as you beat it in. Each 2 oz (50g) of butter will absorb 1 teaspoon of water. You can also do this with margarine for a low calorie dairy spread. See Slimming Hints in Health Matters.

○ **Cheese . . .**

463   To get the best flavour from cheese it should be kept in a cold pantry rather than the fridge. It won't go mouldy if you wrap it in muslin, sprinkle it with vinegar and keep it in a covered, raised dish.
    To stop cheese hardening smear a film of butter round the exposed edges.

464   Dried out cheese will regain its moisture if soaked in buttermilk.

465   Dried up old bits of cheese can be coarse grated and frozen, ready to add to sauces at some later date.

Bread
and Pastry

466   To keep bread fresh, wash and dry a large potato and keep it in the bread bin.

| 467 | Cut bread easily by dipping the knife into boiling water in between slices. |

| 468 | Stale bread can be turned into breadcrumbs in a mixer and popped into bags or small plastic pots for the freezer. |

| 469 | When mincing ingredients for a pâté or meat loaf, finish by processing a slice of bread through the mincing machine to push out the last of the ingredients and help clean the mincer. |

| 470 | Bread which is a day or so old will taste freshly baked again if you run it quickly under the tap – top and bottom – and pop it in a hot oven for no more than a couple of minutes. |

| 471 | Bread won't shrink in baking if you place a tin of water on the floor of the oven. |

| 472 | No more soggy toast if you tap it all over with a spoon before putting it in the toast rack. |

| 473 | Economy bread – buy a 10 oz (275g) packet of bread mix and add 4 oz (100g) of plain, strong flour and a third more of the amount of water stated in the baking instructions on the packet. You should get up to 6 extra rolls. |

| 474 | To give pastry a lighter result and make it quicker to mix, grate hard fat from the fridge before adding to the flour. |

| 475 | For a quick, cheap and easy pastry substitute for pies and flans, mix 8 digestive biscuits with 2 oz (50g) of butter. Pop the biscuits in a blender or crush with a rolling pin. Add melted butter and when mixed turn the crumb base into a flan dish. Press it evenly round sides and bottom. Chill for a few hours and bake at 375°F/190°C (Mark 5) for 15 minutes. |

| 476 | When making pastry which is to be served cold, use milk to moisten it. This way it will keep shorter and crisper longer than if you use water. |

| 477 | Keep a thin polythene bag beside you when making dough. Quickly slip your hand into it to answer the phone and open fridge and cupboard doors. |

478 Flour your hands before working with dough to shape scones and bread. You'll work faster as the dough won't stick to you . . .

479 A milk bottle makes a good stand-in for a rolling pin.

Sweet Things

480 Keep a few cubes of sugar in biscuit tins for ever-crisp biscuits.

481 Place baking sheets containing biscuit mix in the upper third part of the oven to avoid burned bottoms.

482 To salvage stale buns and scones, brush them in milk and pop them in the oven. They'll taste fresh baked when served with butter and jam.

483 Chopped dates are cheaper and as tasty as dried fruit for cakes, puddings, scones and biscuits.

484 For orange and lemon peel flavourings in dried form, pound them up finely when they've been thoroughly dried in the oven and store them in a jar.

485 | Stop a skin forming on newly-boiled custard by sprinkling sugar on top.

486 | When treacle is called for in a recipe, dust the measuring bowl and it won't stick. Or weigh the treacle in the container and remove it by the spoonful until the weight of the tin goes down by the amount you need.

487 | When you need a jelly in a hurry, melt the cubes in just enough boiling water to cover them, stirring until they dissolve. Then gradually add ice-cold water until you make up the stated amount of liquid.

O *Cakes . . .*

488 | When making a fruit cake, the fruit won't sink to the bottom if you dredge the fruit with flour before adding to the cake mix ingredients.

489 | If you have a problem with cakes burning at the bottom, prevent it happening in future by placing the tin inside a larger tin with two sticks across the bottom to raise it slightly.

490 | Economy cake – buy a packet of best quality cake mix, add 3 tablespoons of self-raising flour, one generous tablespoon of caster sugar and the white of an egg. Mix with 3 dessertspoons more of water than recommended in the recipe and now follow the cake instructions for baking. You should get up to a dozen extra small cakes.

491 | Make your own economy cake flavouring using grated or finely chopped orange or lemon peel. Place it in bottles to which you add a good-quality brandy or runny honey and leave the skins to soak in the liquid for several months. Ideal for fruit cakes, Christmas puddings, mince pies etc.

492 | Cake won't go dry if stored in a tight-fitting tin with a couple of slices of bread for company.

493   To remove an iced cake from a cake tin sunny side up and unbroken, store the cake on the lid and place the bottom inverted over it.

494   To remove a cake easily from its tin after baking, place cake and tin in a basin of hot water. The heat will loosen it just sufficiently to be turned out. Do not try this with a loose-bottomed cake tin! Or stand the tin for a few moments on a damp tea-towel and you'll turn the cake out without damaging it.

495   To test if a cake is properly cooked, insert a skewer in the middle. If it comes out cleanly, the cake is ready.

○   *Meringues . . .*

496   For guaranteed 'set firm' meringues, add a teaspoon of cornflour to the sugar before adding the egg whites. Or you could try a pinch of salt or a little cream of tartar.

497   To cut a meringue cleanly coat the knife with butter.

498   If meringues, however hard you try, end up in pieces, arrange them decoratively with lashings of whipped cream and slivers of soft fruit, such as peaches, for an ambrosial pudding.

○ *Jams . . .*

|499| Add a small pat of butter to the fruit when making jam and it won't bubble over.

|500| When fruit juice boils over during jam or pie making, shake salt onto the spill. When burned to a crisp it can be easily scraped up.

|501| If jam is allowed to cool for a few minutes, then given a brisk stir before being decanted into pots, any 'scum' which might have risen will now be absorbed.

|502| Keep wax paper from cereal wrappings for making jam jar seals. Using an upturned glass as a template, fold the paper over as many times as possible and cut a whole lot of circles in one go.

|503| Good quality clingfilm does a good enough job for sealing jam jars.

○ *Sugar . . .*

|504| Don't waste money on caster or icing sugar. The grinder attachment on your blender will convert granulated sugar to caster in a couple of seconds, or to icing sugar if allowed to run for a little longer.

|505| Keep a slice of apple in a cannister of brown sugar and it won't harden.

|506| Brown sugar dried out and set rock hard in a lump can still be used when broken down with a cheese grater.

Miscellaneous

|507| To prevent baking tins rusting, rub with fresh lard and thoroughly heat in the oven before using.

508 To cut out the time-consuming chore of cleaning grill and roasting pans, burners and the base of the oven, line them with kitchen foil.

509 Metal is a fast heat conductor; dishes cooked in china or glass will cook more slowly. Placing a metal tray under a flan dish when baking pies or quiches will speed the heat process through the pastry.

510 Oven to tableware saves time but often the appearance is spoiled by cooking spills. It only takes a couple of seconds to wipe them off with salt on the dampened corner of a tea-towel before serving.

511 Fry in a combination of butter and oil (butter first) and your food is less likely to burn.

512 Add a couple of tablespoons of water to fat in a roasting tin before putting it in the oven to prevent the fat burning.

513 Save mess, blocked sinks and time by pouring hot fat into an empty can. When it sets, it's easy to dispose of – or to keep for another time.

514 If fat must be poured down a sink, always follow it with a good squirt of washing-up liquid and lots of hot water to avoid blockages.

515 To keep recipes etc clean whilst cooking, buy a photo album in the sales. The plastic covers will keep them dry and handy.

516 It saves a lot of time and wasted food later if a cook gets into the habit of tasting and testing food as the cooking is in progress.

517 If you haven't got a cheese slicer, use a potato peeler for thinly slicing cheese. Make your own potato crisps with either slicer or peeler.

518 For picnics, use a nutcracker to break ice into pieces small enough for a thermos flask. For instant crushed ice, put the cubes in a plastic bag and smash with a hammer or the heel of a shoe.

519   Make your own pure barley water without additives by simply putting one teaspoon of washed pearl barley in 2 pints (1.1 litres) of cold water. Bring to the boil and let it stand for 5 minutes to cool. Strain and add the juice of 2 lemons and sugar to taste.

520   A small piece of marrow bone makes a good stand-in for a pie funnel.

521   Keep chopping boards spotlessly clean and free from bacteria by scrubbing in very hot water and bleaching stains with salt or a cut lemon.

522   Save on kitchen gadgets – use the corner of a chopping board and a knife to cream garlic with salt to draw out the juice.

○   *Kitchen fires . . .*

523   If a kitchen fire starts, immediately sprinkle salt or bicarbonate of soda to stop the spread of flames and smoke.

524   If a chip pan catches fire, carefully drape a damp tea-towel over the top to exclude the air.

○   *Substitutes for . . .*

525   When you're out of gravy browning, add a dash of instant coffee.

526   Out of milk? They do say that a small portion of well-beaten egg added to the cup, before pouring in the coffee, is a good substitute.

527   In baking you can replace an egg with a tablespoon of vinegar in a cake mix; the result will be the same but the cost less.

528   When you're short of eggs, a tablespoon of tapioca is a useful standby for the store cupboard. One tablespoon, soaked for a couple of hours in enough water to cover it, will then bind rissoles and meat loves, coat fish etc.

529 If soured cream mentioned in a recipe is unobtainable, double cream with lemon juice added makes a passable standby.

530 A cheap substitute for eggs when coating fish is custard powder mixed in equal proportions with flour.

Easy Entertaining

531 Put clingfilm on polished wood surfaces to avoid water marks from glasses.

532 If ashtrays are given a coat of wax polish, they only need a quick wipe with kitchen towel to clean.

533 To remove candlewax from a table or fabric, rub with an ice cube to harden so that the excess scrapes off easily, then place brown paper or a kitchen towel on top to draw the rest.

534 Burning candles cut down smoke from the atmosphere. Candles kept in the fridge for a few hours before burn more slowly.

535 Coloured napkins may be pretty, but white ones are usually cheaper and when spills occur they won't stain clothes or carpet during well-intentioned mopping up sessions.

536 You can get away with cheaper entertaining if you have a lot of people . . . If space is a problem, have them on consecutive nights. Prepare in advance the same food, just make more of it. You get discounts on wine when you buy in bulk, the flowers will still be fresh, and the house kept easily clean and tidy.

537 Add packets of soup to meat courses to stretch the meal if an unexpected guest arrives.

538 When guests come to stay and you're short of hanging space, a concertina-style wooden clothes drier and coat hangers provides an alternative wardrobe.

539 Take short cuts where possible. To dry large amounts of lettuce for parties, pop the washed leaves into a clean pillowcase and twirl in the spin dryer for a few seconds.

540 For a quick and effortless party dip, stir 2 dessertspoons of dried vegetables into ¼ pint (150 ml) of yoghurt and leave overnight for the mixture to thicken. You can add chives, chopped spring onion or celery, or fold in some sour cream or cottage cheese to change flavour and texture. Season to taste.

O   *Drinks . . .*

541 If you have half an orange or lemon in the fridge, slice it and add it to an ice tray to freeze in cubes for drinks.

542 Even for parties, you don't have to buy extra ice trays. Use the bottom halves of plastic egg boxes half-filled with water.

543 A cheap and refreshing non-alcoholic drink for drivers is soda water with a slice of lemon and a few drops of angostura bitters.

544 Make sure the champagne is properly chilled; if still warm it will shower over everyone as its gases explode.

545 Even an inexpensive red wine, if left uncorked at room temperature for at least 2 hours, will improve in taste.

546   The secret of pouring wine without ruining table linen and dripping on guests is to finish the pouring with a slight rolling action and an upward tilt of the bottle.

547   If percolated coffee has a strong overbrewed taste, add a pinch of salt to take away the bitterness.

Carefree Christmas

548   If the turkey is slow defrosting, speed things up with the aid of a hairdryer.

549   If the power is cut off, barbecue the turkey and eat it by candlelight.

550   Delicious potted turkey or ham can be made in a jiffy by mincing the meat and mixing it with melted butter, salt and pepper and fresh herbs.

551   Soften last year's dried fruit and candied peel by soaking it in boiling water and letting it sit for a couple of minutes.

552   A teaspoon of glycerine added to royal icing stops it becoming too hard.

553   Buy ordinary shop-bought mince pieces, lift their lids and, with a clean meat baster, squirt some brandy or rum into the centres before heating them through in the oven. You can swear you made them yourself!

554   Soak walnuts overnight in salty water – they'll crack easily without smashing the contents of the shell.

555   Store nuts somewhere cool – they become rancid extremely quickly if left in a warm atmosphere. Always taste before using to check.

556   If brazil nuts are placed in a pan of cold water, brought to the boil and after 1 minute plunged back into cold, they'll shell easily with their contents intact.

557   If the fire won't start, get a hairdryer and gently fan the flames. Sprinkle sugar to help the flames spread. Orange peel is a good fire-lighter with a Christmassy smell.

558   If making mulled wine or gaelic coffee, put a metal spoon in the glass before adding hot liquid to avoid cracks and use it again to keep the cream on the surface.

○   *Christmas cakes . . .*

559   To make a pretty average Christmas cake taste like the de-luxe variety, buy it, along with a miniature bottle of decent brandy, about a fortnight before Christmas. Using a thin skewer to poke holes in the cake and add the brandy in drips, getting it as deep into the holes as you can. A few days later, turn it over repeat the procedure on the bottom. Repeat the process at intervals until the bottle is empty.

560   When a Christmas cake is mixed and ready for the oven, cover it with a tea-towel and leave it for 24 hours to get the maximum moisture and flavour.

○   *Christmas puddings . . .*

561   Cold tea rather than beer added to a Christmas pudding mix stops it drying out and gives it a richer colour.

562   To make sure a Christmas pudding boils evenly, put sticks or skewers across the bottom of the pan.

563   If by chance the Christmas pudding turns out like a cannon-ball, slice it and fry it in butter and serve with sugar and cream.

564   To keep the Christmas pudding flaming all the way to the table, heat both the serving plate and the brandy before you ignite it.

○ *Decorating . . .*

565 Collecting pine cones is a healthy festive occupation and gives the house a delightful woody smell. Paint them gold or silver or throw a few on the fire.

566 Make attractive gift labels, or tree decorations, by cutting up last year's Christmas cards with pinking scissors.

567 Buy paper tablecloths with Christmas designs from sales and market stalls and save money by cutting them up for wrapping paper – excellent for larger parcels.

568 Buy the large size rolls of kitchen foil for wrapping parcels, making tree decorations and covering the tree-stand or pot.

569 Cover ping-pong balls in foil for shiny baubles without breakages.

570 Use old egg boxes to cut out dome shapes and wrap in foil for festive bells; tie onto the tree with coloured wool or string through the top.

571 Spray the tree with hair lacquer to slow down the rate at which needles fall.

572 Put a square of red or green material under the tree and simply shake the corners into the middle to collect needles easily, and save clogging the hoover.

Clothes Care

Boots and Shoes

573 Stuff rolled up magazines in tall boots and crumpled newspapers in shoes and sandals to keep their shape.

574 To freshen shoes, boots, wellies or trainers and remove the odour of smelly feet, sprinkle a teaspoon of bicarbonate of soda inside and shake to spread around. Leave them in the open air for a couple of hours if possible.

575 Disguise shabby patches on shoes, such as scuffed heels from driving the car, by touching them up with a matching felt tip or marker pen.

○ *Polishing and cleaning . . .*

576 Save on shoe polish by making your beeswax furniture polish double up as a leather shoe and handbag preserver. The less polish, the better the shine. The secret lies in rubbing it well in and removing every trace from the surface with a polishing brush.

577 Saddle soap in glycerine bars from saddlers makes a cheap shoe cleaner.

578 To remoisten cake shoe polish which has dried out hard, place the sealed tin in a shallow bath of boiling water for a few minutes, then mix the polish with a little turpentine.

579 Clogged up shoe brushes should be washed in warm water and washing soda.

580 Clean patent leather with slightly warm milk, or dip a rag in a little petrol. Give an occasional rub with petroleum jelly to guard against cracking. Polish off with a soft, clean rag.

581 De-stain light coloured shoes by mixing a paste made from petrol and bran and leave it to dry on the shoes for about 10 minutes. Shake it off and dust with a clean damp cloth.

582 To make rubber riding boots look like leather, polish with leather dressing available from saddlers.

583 To blacken brown boots or shoes, first rub them all over with the cut side of a raw potato. Mix equal parts of blue black ink and ordinary shoe black into a creamy paste and use this mixture to polish the leather.

584 Treat new boots or shoes which won't polish by rubbing them over with half a lemon and leave it to dry thoroughly. Repeat when necessary.

○ *Softening and stretching . . .*

585 Brown leather shoes will keep supple given an occasional polish with the inside of a banana skin. Let them dry and polish off with a soft rag.

586   To soften boots and shoes, below-stairs maids applied castor oil to leather to make it more pliable. When worn, the heat of the foot caused the oil to be absorbed by the leather, which was then polished in the ordinary way.

587   To prevent new shoes rubbing, especially sandal straps, rub the leather where it pinches with moist soap.

588   Before throwing out shoes which pinch, try warming them several times over the steam from a kettle, and wear them around the house in between steaming sessions to stretch the leather.

○   *Drying . . .*

589   When shoes or boots get a soaking, dry them away from direct heat and stuff them with newspaper to absorb damp and keep the shape.

590   If shoes or boots get wet apply a few drops of paraffin to your shoe cleaner to help restore the leather.

591   Dry the inside of wellington boots with a hairdryer.

592   To remove sea stains from leather or shoes, melt a small lump of washing soda in some hot milk. Dip a piece of clean sponge in the mixture and rub all over the leather. Put in the sun to dry and shine up with good quality polish.

Tights
and Stockings

593 Boiling tights and odd stockings will produce a potful of neutral coloured ones which can be re-matched.

594 Or put them all in a black dye bath.

595 Old laddered stockings can help save on clothes pegs and prevent making marks on woollens or delicate fabrics. Put stocking through the arms of newly-washed garments and peg to the line.

596 A quick rub with a bar of moist soap or a dab with colourless varnish stops a ladder spreading.

597 Some people will tell you that washing tights in a mild soap solution and not rinsing them will make them less likely to snag or ladder; others that keeping them in the freezer and thawing and dripping dry before using, doubles their life expectancy . . . Take your pick!

Washing and Cleaning

598 Keep your washing-up liquid beside the machine on wash day. A quick squirt on dirty collars, cuffs and other stains as you pop them in, aids the wash.

599 Always test the colour fastness of fabrics by wetting a corner and ironing it between pieces of white cloth.

600 To wash any delicate material where the dye is likely to run, use potato water. See the section on Stain Removal.

601 Unpleasant underarm smells on washable clothes can first be treated with a roll-on deodorant to dampen the affected area, then washed in the usual way and given a final rinse in vinegar and water.

602 Perspiration stains will disappear if a couple of aspirins are dissolved in the washing water.

603 Save pounds on dry-cleaning. After wearing, brush clothes gently and hang them to air, preferably out of doors, and sponge trouble spots where shine or perspiration weakens the material, with a weak salt and vinegar solution.

604 Retexture coat collars and hat brims to remove grease with a cloth dipped in ammonia. This is also suitable for velvet, but hold the garment in front of a hot iron afterwards to draw the pile. Try a little shampoo on dampened cotton wool round a hat band, but follow with a clean pad and a few drops of vinegar to removal all traces of soap. Alternatively, rub the brim with Fuller's Earth and leave overnight to absorb the grease – the safest dry-cleaning method.

605 Mud stained umbrellas can be cleaned by rubbing with methylated spirits on a rag.

606 Silk umbrellas need gentler treatment. Put a tablespoon of sugar in a basin and pour a pint of boiling water over it. Once the sugar dissolves, open the umbrella and starting at the tip or ferule, wash down each section drawing the sponge in a straight line to the edge. Hang the open umbrella in the fresh air to dry.

607 Keep a small phial of petrol – the kind you buy at tobacconists as lighter fuel – in your cleaning kit. It's cheaper for instant cleaning than the fancy brand bottles and cans. Where remedies mention petrol or benzine, this is the type to use.

○ *Lace . . .*

608 Cover lace with clean white tissue paper before ironing to prevent a shiny look.

609 White lace or silk which has seen better days can be dyed to a lovely creamy beige if you soak it for about 5 minutes in a bowl of water to which you've added 2 cups of strong black coffee with a few teaspoons of sugar in it. Keep the solution moving around the material to avoid patchiness in the dye. Rinse and dry off the surplus quickly by rolling in a bath towel.

610 Dusky lace which should really be white can be soaked in sour milk before washing to lighten it. If you don't have sour milk, add a few drops of lemon to fresh milk, give it a good stir, and let it sit awhile before using.

○ *Velvet . . .*

611 If velvet riding hats are faded, immerse in a bucket containing a cold water dye solution and prop on a pole to dry.

|612| Hang a crushed velvet garment over a hot bath so the steam can take out the creases. Steam a velvet hat over a kettle.

○ *Taffeta* . . .

|613| To clean taffeta, soak it in tepid water in which 2 tablespoons of salt have been dissolved, then wash in lukewarm water and pure soap. To stiffen, add ½ a teaspoon of borax to the rinsing water. Do not wring, and iron before completely dry.

○ *Suede and kid* . . .

|614| Haberdashery departments sell 'suede renovating cloths'. They are very expensive and on closer inspection look like very fine sandpaper. Buy fine sandpaper at a fraction of the cost, wrap a piece round a cork block, and clean the suede by rubbing gently in one direction only.

|615| To renovate suede cuffs and collars, use a soft brush, such as a baby's hair brush, dip it in petrol and rub the worn areas until all the dirt is removed.

616 | Where suede handbags have acquired greased and stained edges, rub the affected parts with a fine emery board.

617 | Suede and kid gloves should be immersed in a bowl of petrol and hung on a line to dry, away from sunlight. Or rub them with fine oatmeal or warm flour, or spot clean with india rubber.

○ **Woollens . . .**

618 | Woollens which have shrunk can be restored to their original size and fluffiness by finishing off a wash with clean soap suds instead of clear water.

619 | Never rub woollens; squeeze gently in lukewarm water.

620 | Knitwear starts to look old if it rubs and forms furry baubles. Stop this happening by turning sweaters inside out before washing, and only lightly press the wool on the wrong side. Try careful shaving with a razor to remove stray fluff.

Ironing

621 | Clothes which have become too dry for ironing should be lightly sprayed with water, rolled up and placed in a plastic bag for an hour.

622 | If you iron while standing on a pillow you'll get through the work quicker – the pillow takes the strain off your back and legs.

623 | To encourage a hem line to disappear, dampen it with white vinegar on a sponge.

624 | To restore the finish on shiny trouser seats when pressing, again use vinegar.

625 | Clothes will look professionally pressed if the iron is first placed over a damp cloth and then over brown paper, which, as it draws the moisture out, firms the materials and counteracts bagginess.

626 When pressing pleats, slip a piece of paper or thin cardboard between the fold and the material underneath to avoid leaving an imprint of the iron.

Recycling

627 Rummage at jumble sales for old-fashioned lace doilys. Wash them, starch them stiffly and cheer up a plain dress with lacy collars and cuffs, or pocket trim.

628 Cut the legs off old jeans and snip upwards with scissors at half inch (12mm) intervals for trendy, frayed shorts, or simply hem them to the required length.

629 Discarded sleeves of woollies make terrific leg warmers.

630 Next to unravelling jumpers bought for a song at jumble sales, the cheapest wool for knitters comes at a vast reduction on shop prices if you send for it by mail order.

631 To recycle jumble sale wool, unpick the garment carefully, winding it first into balls then into skeins around a frame made from a metal coat hanger. Wash it in lukewarm water, then shake the excess off and allow the wool to dry naturally before rewinding in balls.

632 Sometimes a coat looks fine from the outside, but a stained and frayed lining lets it down. Unpick the old lining, press it flat and use it as a pattern to cut out a new one. Or scour the jumble sales for a coat in your size where the nearly-new lining is its best feature.

633 Old summer dresses make kitchen aprons with huge pockets.

634 Hoard buckles, buttons and good zips from cast-off clothing and find old and expensive sets of buttons on unfashionable jumble sale clothes.

635 Men's ties which are no longer in fashion can make lovely belts with the addition of a stiffener and buckle. Or decorate a plain felt hat with a tie band.

636   Clear nail varnish dabbed sparingly around buttonholes, and
the ends of ribbon will stop them fraying.

O   *Shirts . . .*

637   Old white shirts, however worn at the cuffs and neck, can be
bleached to freshen them and the backs cut away and used to
make pillowcases.

638   When a shirt is stained beyond redemption, unpick the collar
and keep it to replace another shirt collar which becomes too
frayed to wear. A blouse or shirt with the frayed collar
removed can often continue life with a granny collar conver-
sion. Or cut a strip off the tail, fold this over and attach it to the
neck in a concertina pleat for a fashionable frilly necked
blouse.

Miscellaneous

639   Thread beads or pearls the easy way using dental floss, and
knot in between each one.

640   To hold the end of a belt in place, use double-sided Sellotape
or adhesive pads from stationers – even try chewing gum in an
emergency.

641   Keep shoulder straps in place by sewing a loop of ribbon into
the shoulder seam of your top and attaching a snap fastener to
the ends. This loop can then be slotted around a bra strap.

O   *Zips . . .*

642   When a zip fastener is broken near the base, pull the slide
down until it comes just below the broken teeth. Cut out the
damaged part. Pull the slide carefully and evenly to engage the
teeth up the two sides. Once past the broken bit, make a new
and firm base by stitching across securely.

643   If you find pulling up a back zip a problem, thread a long shoe lace through the hole in the zip and hoist it up.

644   Revive old zips by spraying them with starch or, if a zip won't run easily, rub over it a few times with the point of a lead pencil. It's the graphite that does the trick.

○   *Storage . . .*

645   To guard against moths in clothes which are to be stored away, after airing and brushing wrap in newspaper and store tightly in boxes sealed with gummed paper.

646   Hang bags of dried orange peel and lavender in loops around coat-hangers in your wardrobe. Clothes smell great and moths will stay clear.

Sewing Box

647   Cheap sewing thread is false economy; it will be forever breaking.

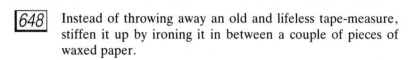

648   Instead of throwing away an old and lifeless tape-measure, stiffen it up by ironing it in between a couple of pieces of waxed paper.

649   Champagne corks are handy for protecting the ends of small scissors and knitting needles.

650   Pull out tacking threads quickly with a crochet hook or eyebrow tweezers.

651   Thread won't get in a tangle so easily if, when you hand sew, you knot the ends separately rather than together.

652   Keep metal fruit jar rings to team with a rubber band to provide a travelling embroidery frame.

653   Dental floss is the answer for a strong hold when sewing on big buttons or those which take the strain on jeans etc – it's virtually impossible to break.

654   When you sew on buttons, paint the thread with colourless varnish to stop fraying.

655   To sew buttons without straining the material, place a matchstick over the button and sew over the stick to secure it. Remove the matchstick and wind the shank of the button with the thread, securing it in the usual way. The button will stay on longer than if sewn without a shank.

656   When mending the fingers of gloves, put a thimble on your finger before you put it into the glove to avoid pricking your fingers.

657   It will be much easier to take up a hem if you press the fabric first at the new level.

○   *Needles . . .*

658   Sharpen blunt sewing needles by stabbing or sewing through sandpaper several times.

659 A see-through plastic toothbrush container stores crochet needles.

660 When threading a needle, you'll see better if you hold it in front of white cloth.

○ *Sewing machines . . .*

661 Secondhand re-conditioned sewing machines from major retailers are generally bargains.

662 Stretched sewing machine belts, placed in cold water for 30 minutes and hung in strong sun, should become taut again.

663 Old felt tip pens are excellent for cleaning fluff from awkward places in sewing machines.

Health Matters

First Aid

664 To shift a fish bone that's lodged in the throat, suck the juice of half a lemon.

665 A piece of cut onion wrapped round a wasp sting reduces pain and swelling.

666 For bruises, apply neat vinegar on a cotton wool pad and bandage to the affected part until the dressing is dry.

667 One of the best sunburn coolers is bicarbonate of soda made into a paste and covered with a light dressing to exclude air.

668 Eyes which are red and inflamed will get instant relief when splashed with ice cold water. Use an eye bath and gently open the eyes in the water.

669 Feeling dizzy? Press a thumbnail into the spot midway between the nostrils and upper lip.

○ *Burns and scalds . . .*

|670| The white of an egg is good for slight burns in an emergency, but cold water, for all but the most extensive burns, is usually the quickest and most effective remedy.

|671| Cover scald immediately with white petroleum jelly and wrap in cotton wool or bandage to exclude the air and prevent blisters and scarring.

Care of the Sick

|672| To cure an attack of biliousness, mix together and sip the juice of one lemon, ½ teaspoon of bicarbonate of soda and 2 or 3 tablespoons of boiling water.

|673| To keep the weight off an injured limb, cut a child's hoop into halves, uniting them in a cross with string or wire. Bind the jagged bits with strips of old soft rag to avoid tears in the bedclothes.

|674| To prevent bed sores and to get rid of the rashes often caused by them, a daily bed bath in a warm salt and water solution is the answer.

○ *Medicine taking . . .*

|675| Numb the tongue with an ice cube before swallowing unpleasant medicine.

|676| To quickly crush a pill, press it firmly between the bowls of 2 teaspoons.

Coughs and Colds

|677| For colds and chills have a hot mustard bath before bed and a warm drink once under the covers.

678 If you're tired and shivery, ward off a cold by soaking in a hot bath into which you've dissolved a handful of salt.

679 For a simple cough mixture – mix equal parts of lemon juice, runny honey and cod liver oil. Adults take a tablespoon when troubled, children a teaspoon. Make in small quantities at a time to ensure freshness.

680 For cold sores, rub on lemon juice, or honey . . .

Aches and Pains

681 To cure cramp in the legs in bed, take half a tumbler of warm water into which you've dissolved a teaspoon of salt.

682 At the onset of a headache, dip a handkerchief in vinegar and place it on the forehead to ease the pain.

683 Gardeners massage aching joints with elder leaves at the end of the day. It is said to give considerable relief to arthritis sufferers.

Lotions and Potions

684 A few drops of vinegar in a tumblerful of water makes a cheap and effective mouthwash for bleeding or ulcerated gums.

685 Fine varicose veins diminish with applications of neat cider vinegar.

686 No need for expensive eye lotions. A teaspoon of bicarbonate of soda to a pint of warm water is just as effective for bathing itchy eyes.

687   To prevent gnat and midge bites, dab oil of lavender or oil of geranium around ankles, wrists and other favourite targets.

688   Cure hiccups by pressing the thumb of the right hand into the palm of the left. Hold your breath. If they persist swallow a teaspoon of vinegar.

689   For an attack of indigestion, don't reach for expensive antacid tables, try a cupful of boiled water sipped slowly, or a few teaspoons of neat lemon juice.

Energy Boosters

690   Do without coffee and tea too if you drink a lot of it, and watch your energy level soar.

691   Have the occasional semi-fast for a day on mineral water and grapes to get rid of toxins.

Hands and Feet

692   For chapped and red hands, mix Vaseline with boracic powder, two thirds to one third.

693   An old fashioned cure for a whitlow – cut a lemon in half and put your finger in the lemon. Bandage both together. Don't keep the lemon on the finger for more than 10 or 12 hours, but then change the dressing and repeat the procedure for as long again. The pain and the whitlow will have gone.

694   To strengthen weak ankles, rub on a salt solution – 1 teaspoon of salt to 1 pint of warm water – at regular intervals. Start by using it morning and evening.

695 To treat corns, soak some bread in vinegar for two days and bind this poultice to the corn overnight. Every 3 days, soak the feet in hot water and peel off a layer of the corn. Continue until it has disappeared.

○ *Chilblains . . .*

696 Chilblains bathed in water in which celery has been boiled, helps get rid of them quickly. Or rub with a lemon and sprinkle powdered aspirin in the toes of socks or stockings.

697 For unbroken chilblains, stir a teaspoon of mustard into ½ pint (300 ml) of turpentine and allow it to sit for a day before rubbing on the chilblains.

Beauty and the Budget

○ *Face and body . . .*

698 To save fortunes and improve your skin beyond belief, cut out smoking, alcohol, tea and coffee. Substitute herbal teas, fruit juice and mineral water.

699 Drink half a glass of lemon juice in water first thing in the morning for clear eyes and complexion; it's an internal cleanser.

700 Make your own mouthwash and breath fresheners. A handful of lavender steeped in boiling water and strained when cool makes a cheap and pleasant mouthwash and gargle. Chewing fresh parsley, cardomom seeds, or coffee beans, or cider vinegar in warm water, are other tried and tested remedies for stale or garlicky breath. Alternatively suck a slice of lemon, skin, pith, pips and all.

701 Boiled parsley allowed to cool, then strained and bottled makes a good skin tonic for all skin types. Keep in the fridge.

702 Cucumber makes a potent astringent. Make your own by peeling, chopping and mashing a cucumber into 2 tablespoons of cold water. Strain, bottle and chill in the fridge. Leave it on the skin for a minute or two before wiping off with damp cotton wool.

703 Cucumber slices on the eyes reduces puffiness. So do tea bags cooled in the fridge, and a bandage dipped in equal parts of rosewater and witch hazel, well chilled, make a soothing eye mask. Lie down in a darkened room for an hour for the full benefit.

704 An ideal skin tonic for dry skin is 8 fl ozs (230 ml) rosewater mixed with 1 tablespoon of liquid honey.

705 An inexpensive nourishing cream for dry skin simply involves putting 1 part rosewater and 2 of glycerine in a bottle and shaking well to mix before each application. Alternatively try neat liquid paraffin.

706 For the benefits of a facial without the drawback of the bill, do a home face treatment. Add some menthol crystals to a bowl of very hot water. Drape a towel over your head and the bowl as you bend over it about 8–10 inches (20–25 cm) from the water. Taking deep breaths, let the steam and menthol vapours unclog your pores and nasal passages. Blot the skin with a tissue before nourishing with face cream, or even apply olive oil to face and neck.

707 You can make any amount of face packs with fruit which has become too soft to eat. Strawberries, which are astringent, are

particularly good on their own or mixed with a little natural yoghurt. Other soft fruit, such as pears and peaches, can be mixed with a little cream for dry skins.

708   A refining face mask only needs a ½ tablespoon of fine oatmeal (grind the coarse kind in a blender) mixed to a paste with a teaspoon of honey and a little warm water.

709   Leftover egg white on its own or mixed with oatmeal makes the perfect face mask for moistening the skin and closing the pores.

710   Or try a facial wash with a ½ tablespoon of oatmeal (finely ground) mixed in the palm of the hand with a little warm water. Massage gently into the skin, rinse and pat dry.

711   Freckles and liver spots will gradually fade if you make up a lotion of equal parts lemon juice, glycerine, olive oil and sour milk and apply at night.

712   As glycerine is sticky, change the formula for hands and body with 4 parts rosewater, 2 of glycerine and 1 of lemon juice. Most natural recipes will store for up to 2 weeks in the fridge.

713   Put your elbows in the skins of 2 lemon halves and rub the inside of avocado skins on your face and neck when you've nourished your inner-self with the contents. You may look and smell like a salad but afterwards you'll have soft white elbows and not a trace of dryness on your face.

714   For a cheap and beneficial body oil and water softener, add a few drops of sunflower oil to the bath . . .

715   For an invigorating herbal bath, substitute the toe from an old stocking or tights for the customary muslin bag, and fill it with water softening oatmeal, plus a few sprigs of herbs or a slice of lemon – even a a few pine needles – and soak in the scented water.

716   Add unwanted perfume to a cheap bottle of baby oil, shake well and add a few drops of this home-brewed bath oil to the water when running the bathwater.

○ *Feet . . .*

717 Sore feet cause wrinkles. A blissful footbath only requires a washing-up bowl with hot water and a lump of washing soda dissolved in it. The soda reduces inflammation and at the same time softens cuticles and corns.

718 After a foot bath, treat your feet once a week to a massage with a little warm olive oil.

○ *Hands and nails . . .*

719 For a cheap barrier cream, smear petroleum jelly on the hands before tackling garden or housework. Run the nails along a moist bar of soap to prevent dirt becoming ingrained from really grubby jobs.

720 This is a handsoftener which is particularly good for people whose hands do heavy or dirty work. Mix equal quantities of olive oil, soap flakes and granulated sugar and beat until the soap flakes dissolve. After rubbing well in, rinse off in warm water.

721 To keep nails from splitting and cracking, paint them with lemon juice 3 times a day and brush them over with strong alum water (from a chemist) before getting into bed. Or soak the fingertips in a cup of warm water and a tablespoon of bicarbonate of soda, mixed. When dry, apply hand cream or olive oil.

722 For superhard nailtips, apply superglue to the absolute edges, being very careful to avoid contact with the skin.

723 Nail varnish often becomes too thick to apply evenly when the bottle is nowhere near empty. Add a few drops of varnish remover, stand it for a few minutes in boiling water, then give it a good shake. It will now go miles further . . .

○ *Hair . . .*

724 Eggs are a well known nourishing treatment for dry or brittle hair. Mix with a little cider vinegar and leave on the head for 15 minutes. Use only warm not hot water to rinse, otherwise you'll cook the egg.

725 Vinegar in the rinsing water adds a shine to brown hair . . .

726 Blondes have for generations used camomile to enhance fair hair and delay greyness.

727 Dispense with hair sprays and shiners. Flyaway hair can be kept in check by rubbing handcream into the palms of the hands and smoothing just a trace onto the hair before brushing through.

728 For a cheap hair conditioner for split ends, take a tablespoon of homemade mayonnaise and massage it into the ends. Cover with a warm towel and let it penetrate the hair for 30 minutes.

729 For a scalp treatment and conditioner, mix 2 tablespoons olive oil, 1 teaspoon of lemon or vinegar and 2 teaspoons of honey and massage in. After 30 minutes rinse and shampoo.

730 Both olive oil and coconut oil are highly regarded in many countries as promotors of hair growth.

731 Where greasy hair is a problem, add a tablespoon of cider vinegar to the final rinse.

732 Make a styling lotion for greasy hair. Roughly chop an entire lemon, boil it in a cup of water until reduced by about half, add a teaspoon of vodka, strain and decant into a plastic spray.

733 To banish dandruff, mix equal parts of vinegar and water, part the hair in sections and apply the lotion on cotton wool, rubbing it well into the scalp. Sit with a towel round your head for 10 minutes, then shampoo.

734 The sun's natural bleaching process can be accelerated by rubbing neat lemon juice on streaks with a pad of cotton wool. Let it dry in the sun for the effect of salon highlights, but follow with a conditioner to counteract the drying effect.

735 To take stains off your skin when home tinting hair, dampen cotton wool with shampoo and dip this into cigarette ash. It removes the colour immediately.

○ *Make-up . . .*

736 Petroleum jelly not only removes mascara from lashes, but leaves them glossy and promotes thick growth.

737 Use petroleum jelly as a lipgloss and to brush on straggly eyebrows to keep them in shape.

738 Instead of expensive cleaners, use sunflower oil to remove face and eye make-up.

739 For an extra squeeze from a make-up (or toothpaste) tube, heat it in hot water before you remove the cap. You'll squeeze out the very last drop this way.

740 Shop at art shops for make-up brushes. You'll get a wide choice of inexpensive ones, but as they weren't intended for the face, wash them well before using and let them sit for a minute in fabric or hair conditioner for extra softness.

741 A lipstick brush pays for itself in no time. You can use every bit of the stub and get a perfect outline and professional finish at the same time.

742 If mascara has apparently dried in its container, make sure it's watertight and leave in hot water for a few minutes.

743 If you drop a cake of eye shadow, pound the broken bits to a powder and apply with a brush.

744 Don't despair if a lipstick breaks in half, melt the broken ends gently over the heat from a candle, press them together and mould the shape with your fingers. Re-set by leaving in the fridge to harden.

Slimming Hints

○ *Exercise and incentives . . .*

745 Get up earlier to play the exercise video, go for a brisk walk or reap the benefits of a public swimming pool when it's less busy. You won't work out as well at the end of the day when you're tired.

746 Keep the exercise bicyle where you can cycle through the TV news bulletins – but not the food commercials. (Avoid all reminders!)

747 After exercise, relax the muscles and restore energy by adding a handful or two of coarse Epsom salts to your hot bath water. This was a popular slimming aid at one time.

748 Keep on the move; boredom leads to eating for something to do. Gardening burns up 300 calories an hour and really stretches and tones the body. If you don't have a garden, why not get an allotment?

749 Don't wear comfortable clothes 'until the weight comes off'. Wear the skirt that won't do up at the waist or the sweater that shows the awful midriff tyres to remind you to keep at it.

750 Cut out a magazine picture of someone you'd like to look like and stick it on the fridge door – it may even be you some time ago. Or how about a nice portrait of a pig if you're an animal lover?

○ **Diet . . .**

751 Lessen your appetite by drinking lemon or herbal tea, black coffee or water, 30 minutes before each meal.

752 It curbs the appetite if you start every meal with a piece of fresh fruit or unsweetened stewed prunes or apricots.

753 If you have to eat out a lot, have at least one other meal that day of apples and water or grapes and water at home.

754 A whole day on the 'one variety of fruit plus water' menu can help you lose up to 3 lbs (1.4 kg) – and is good for the system.

755 After breakfast, peel carrots, celery or cucumber into sticks, sprinkle with salt and lemon and cover with clingfilm for the fridge. When you must snack between meals, have them with a glass of mineral water.

| 756 | Keep your frying and chip pans at the home of a good friend if you can't be trusted! |

| 757 | Fad diets develop cravings. You could eat anything you want and *still* lose weight if you use a small dinner plate and put on it only half of your 'normal' portion. |

| 758 | Weight watchers succeed because for one thing, you diet in company. Diet with a friend, set targets, compare progress daily. Treat yourself to a day out, lunch and clothes shopping, or an all-in day package at a health farm when goals are reached. |

| 759 | Get a good pair of scales and a calorie chart and check everything that goes in your mouth. You are saving money by eating less and looking better. |

| 760 | If you can't bear salad without dressing, try a spoon of natural low fat yoghurt with a squeeze of lemon juice. |

| 761 | Hardboiled eggs take some time to digest, and are therefore good for staving off hunger pangs. Easy for counting calories too, one size 3 egg is a straight 2 oz (50g) of protein. |

| 762 | Make a cheap, low fat dairy spread: cut 8 oz (225g) hard margarine into small cubes and gradually beat 4 fl oz (125 ml) of warm water into it until absorbed. Pot in tubs. This is 140 calories per ounce – it was 208 before you stretched it. |

| 763 | Take time to prepare salads and other slimming foods as attractively as possible. A fruit kebab looks wonderful. |

| 764 | Make low-calorie soft drinks special by using your best glass, ice and a twist of lemon. |

| 765 | If all else fails, resolve to cut out just one fattening thing from your diet. Whether you substitute sweeteners for sugar in tea or coffee or low fat spread for butter, in time it will pay. |

| 766 | Fat children grow into fat adults, so help train yours now by increasing the amount of salad and fruit you buy – paid for by the amount you save on cakes, biscuits and sweets. |

767   With 6 small meals a day, you'll feel less hungry and burn up
more calories than you previously did on 3 bigger ones.

Green Fingers

Garden
Equipment

768 Plastic squash bottles with their bottoms cut off, act as mini-cloches for young plants like courgettes or lettuces. Push them well into the ground to protect them from cutworms and slugs. Later, unscrew the tops to acclimatise the plants to colder air.

769 Old stockings or tights, the more laddered the better, are just the thing for storing bulbs. Hang them in a cool dry place. You can store a glut of onions in this way too.

770 Cut up stockings and tights in strips to make useful ties for garden and greenhouse plants. The 'stretch' in them won't restrict growth.

771 Keep an old plastic jiffy lemon juice container in the green-house for watering tender young seedlings drop by drop with-out damaging the shoots.

772 Don't buy special seed trays. Cardboard egg boxes make excellent peat containers for young seedlings, one per compartment. The box can go straight into the ground when planting out, as the cardboard will disintegrate.

773 Plastic food containers – yoghurt, cottage cheese tubs etc– with drainage holes punched in the bottom are as good as flower pots for cuttings.

774 Construct a makeshift greenhouse for early planting, with heavy duty polythene attached to stout canes and placed at an angle against a sheltered wall.

775 Don't buy supporting canes for young plants. Use lengths of twigs and branches, which will look less conspicuous as the plants grow through them.

776 Old potato peelers make useful gadgets for removing weeds from a lawn.

777 A pair of gardening gloves will give longer service if spare left-hand ones are washed and turned inside out (the right-handed glove generally wears out first). When finished with, rubber gardening gloves can make tough elastic bands by cutting strips from the wrists and fingers.

778 Mend a garden hose with an off-cut of copper piping. Cut out the damaged part, immerse the newly cut ends in hot water to stretch them and insert the piping to fill the gap.

779 Once your garden hose has too many holes in it to make it repairable, add a few more and turn it into a sprinkler for lawn or vegetable patch.

Planting and Tending

780 Never plant gladioli near a vegetable patch as they'll have an ill effect on peas and beans and fatal consequences for strawberries.

|781| Nettles do a good job in stimulating the growth of neighbouring plants. Pick the tops from very young nettles and cook for a delicious vegetable not unlike spinach.

|782| Nettles speed up the decomposing process of a compost heap and if young fruit trees or bushes are planted in the spot where nettles have been dug up, they'll have instant enriched nursery beds.

|783| Foxgloves keep disease at bay, both when planted near vegetables and herbs or flowers in the garden.

|784| You can alter the colour of hydrangeas without buying new plants by sprinkling lime around the plant for pink, and adding a tablet of aluminium sulphate to the watering can for blue.

|785| Increase your yield of sweet peas by placing crushed eggshells under the seeds when planting.

|786| Plant geraniums in an old-fashioned enamel sink mounted on bricks.

|787| If a lawn becomes really overgrown, cut the length of the grass back in stages. The shock if severely cut back makes it less sturdy and it will then need fertiliser to stimulate the growth.

|788| Pinch out the top of broad beans when the pods start to come, you'll now have an extra and palatable vegetable when lightly boiled.

|789| Cross the supporting canes for runner beans no more than halfway up their height from ground level. The beans will then hang outwards for quick and easy picking.

|790| Watering the leaves of runner beans (and sweet peas) as well as the soil during very dry weather is essential for a bumper crop . . .

|791| Parsley can be difficult to grow from seed unless you pour boiling water on it before sowing to speed the germination process.

792   Only use organic compost from your waste – grass mowings, nettles, kitchen refuse etc – and place wet newspaper under new plants as they are put in the ground.

793   Organic vegetables are expensive in the shops, but not many people have the space for growing their own. Perhaps an elderly person in your area with room to spare for a vegetable plot would agree to you doing the work and sharing the produce.

○ *Fertilisers . . .*

794   Banana skins baked in the oven and dug under the soil around rose beds add potassium-rich goodness for vigorous growth.

795   Beer is a drink that hollyhocks love, it's the yeast that works wonders.

796   1 oz (25g) of Epsom salts in a gallon (4.5 litres) of water every few weeks is a cheap and efficacious tonic for rose bushes.

797   Save dried tea and coffee bags. Open them up and sprinkle them on the lawn for an instant fertiliser.

798   Bury old leather boots and shoes in the garden rather than chuck them in the dustbin. When the leather eventually rots down it adds all manner of nutrients to the soil.

799   For an even better show of irises next year, sprinkle Epsom salts in crystal form round their rhizomes in the summer.

800   Tea leaves make the perfect mulch for camellias.

801   Mix dry mustard with fertiliser as bulbs are planted to make daffodils a brighter yellow.

Diseases and Pests

802   Moth repellent rings hung from peach trees stops leaf curl which blights them.

○ *Insects . . .*

| 803 | French marigolds are like nursemaids. Their good 'vibrations' drive whitefly from plants like roses and tomatoes, peppers and aubergines. |

| 804 | Water roses, cabbages and other delicacies which greenfly crave with leftover washing-up liquid to keep the greenfly at bay. |

| 805 | Garlic planted round rose bushes is another greenfly deterrent. |

| 806 | Kill aphids with a cheap DIY rhubarb spray: Chop 3 lbs (1.4kg) of rhubarb leaves, place in 6 pints (3.4 litres) of water and boil for an hour. Strain the liquid, and when cool add a solution of 1 oz (25g) of soap flakes dissolved in 2 pints (1.1 litres) of warm water. When well mixed, it's ready to spray. |

| 807 | Flies and mosquitoes hate mint. Rub a fresh sprig on your exposed parts before working in the garden. |

| 808 | Wasps for some reason are attracted to moth balls. Place some in an open trap away from their nest, to draw them out. |

○ *Creatures . . .*

| 809 | If you scatter mustard powder around blooms, it stops the ravages of worms. |

| 810 | A large nail stuck in the ground next to tomato plants is said to keep cutworms away. |

| 811 | Fill shallow pots with beer to trap slugs. It's kinder to hedgehogs too who may become tipsy, but they won't be killed by lethal slug pellets. |

| 812 | When moles play havoc with your manicured lawn, try putting a handful of coffee grounds in their runs. |

813 Squirrels and rabbits don't find moth balls much to their taste, so scatter a few round tomato plants and other edibles.

814 Crush a few moth balls around flower beds and dogs will do a U-turn at the first whiff.

815 Dried orange or lemon peel, crumbled and scattered around bedding plants, will deter cats. So will a bicycle tyre (the IQ of the cat is not thought to be high and the theory is that they think it's a snake!).

816 Mice won't go near peas or beans if the seeds are soaked in paraffin before planting – about 30 minutes will do.

○ *Weeds . . .*

817 Buying table salt in bulk and sprinkling it in between paving stones will kill unwanted grass.

818 Make useful mulches to prevent weeds germinating and to keep in moisture, from old carpet anchored with stones, or heavy black polythene such as dustbin liners, or thick layers of newspaper approximately ½ inch (1 cm) or cardboard overlapping and weighted at the edges.

819   To cut down weeding time, avoid using grass cuttings as a mulch when the grass is seeding.

Plants on the House

○   *Tending and welfare . . .*

820   A few drops of castor oil fed to the soil every 6 weeks will make houseplants greener.

821   When planting geraniums, add coffee grounds to the compost to increase growth.

822   Save coffee grounds and tea leaves for mixing with houseplant compost. Ferns will be especially appreciative.

823   Ferns will stay a healthy bright green given a dose of ammonia – a teaspoon to a quart (2 pints/1 litre) of water.

824   Water your plants with leftover tea. They will benefit from the boiled water and the fact that it's more likely to be tepid than stone cold which chills plants.

825   Bring a poinsettia into bloom again next Christmas by putting a black dustbin liner over it at night to protect it from artificial light.

826   Don't throw out extendable curtain rods, they provide the ideal support for tall plants and as the plant shoots up you can lengthen the rod.

827   Leaving an apple core in the centre of an urn plant will force it to flower.

828   It's an established fact that plants respond better to owners who talk to them and stroke them. If you're still not convinced, take two identical species of young plants from cuttings. Give one the special treatment daily and not the other.

The one that is stroked and has nice things whispered in its ear will, in a short time, look sturdier.

829 | Tip from a well-known Dutch flower grower. Never thank someone for a plant as if it's an inanimate object – you'll hurt its feelings and it won't do well for you.

830 | Plants like company, keep them in groups and spray above them very lightly to help them build up their own greenhouse atmosphere.

831 | Never move a plant once it's doing well in a certain spot, but turn it round regularly for even growth, otherwise it will lean towards the light.

832 | Only keep houseplants on windowsills at night in winter if there are blinds. Window areas that are shut off by curtains, will kill plants by trapping cold air around them.

833 | If you're given an African violet, but don't have the sunny windowsill which they love, keep it under a tablelamp and leave the light on at night.

834 | Water hanging baskets by placing ice cubes on top of the soil. This will stop them dripping everywhere.

|835| Try the water from boiled eggs (when cooled) on your African violets and watch them bloom from the added calcium.

|836| Rinse milk bottles with water and pour on houseplants to provide free plant food.

|837| To improve the colour of plants which have become pale and anaemic-looking add a teaspoon of Epsom salts, preferably to rainwater, at their next drink.

|838| Don't spend money on expensive leafshine for houseplants, polish them in skimmed milk, never olive oil as some recommend for rubberplants etc, it only clogs the pores and attracts the dirt.

○ *Planting and potting . . .*

|839| Mix charcoal pieces with soil at the base of plant pots. It keeps the soil sweet and aids drainage.

|840| To efficiently re-pot a plant, take the empty pot in which the plant has been growing and place it inside the one into which the plant is to go. Pack compost tightly into the space between the pots. Remove the inner pot, place the plant in its immaculately tailored space and firm round.

|841| If a plant sticks when you are trying to get it out of the pot, try a push from underneath with a pencil through the drainage hole.

|842| Speed up the start of date and peach trees by soaking the stones for a couple of days in a cup of water.

|843| Halves of grapefruit skins filled with compost make good beds for indoor seedlings.

844   If you don't have pots to spare, put moist compost in a transparent polythene bag, insert seeds, pips or stones in the soil and tie the bag securely. Put the bag in the airing cupboard until shoots appear.

845   Propagating cases are an unnecessary expense. Put up to 6 stem cuttings (depending on how big they are) into a well-scrubbed pot of peaty compost. With a couple of sticks in the soil, make a tent by covering the pot with a polythene bag and keep them at no less than 16°C, 60°F.

846   Never handle seedlings by the stems or you'll bruise them. Only touch the leaves using a pointed stick to lightly separate the roots.

847   You will increase the life expectancy of potted plants if you remember that sand makes soil lighter but lets plants dry out more quickly, and that peat increases the soil's capacity to retain moisture. A mixture is ideal. Plants in porous terracotta pots need more frequent watering than those in plastic pots. Plastic pots are more likely to become waterlogged if the plant is given more than it needs to drink.

○   *Pests and diseases . . .*

848   Greenfly seem greatly attracted to begonias and other tasty houseplants. A clove of garlic embedded in the soil will ensure that the attraction is short-lived.

849   When a plant has a pest infestation, isolate it and spray with a solution of soap and water – it should do the trick.

850   Keep African violets free from stem rot by standing them in a bowl of water for about an hour for a good drink. Never water this plant from the top. Stand the pot on coarse sand to provide a moist atmosphere which will then be absorbed by the leaves.

851   Sickly plants, if they're going to die, go downhill fast. It's often best to salvage the top and treat it as a cutting before it's too late.

○ **When away . . .**

852 When you go on holiday, soak a thick bath towel with water and leave your well-watered houseplants sitting on this. They will absorb just enough extra moisture to keep going. Don't stand them in water as the roots will become waterlogged and rot. (Wet newspapers, although more messy, will do as well. Filling the bath with enough water to just cover a layer of bricks on which you then stand the plants, also gives them all the moisture they need.)

853 Denuding windowsills of plants is often a good indicator to burglars that you have gone on holiday. Some plants such as sanseveria or Mother-in-Law's Tongue actually thrive on neglect and appreciate drier conditions and will act as visible watchplants in your absence.

○ **Plants for free . . .**

854 Take cuttings from an overgrown rubberplant to provide luxury presents for friends at little cost to you. Strip a piece of bark from around the stem 8 inches (20 cm) from the top of the plant. Cover this stripped section with a ball of moist sphagnum moss, wrap in clingfilm and secure to make an airtight polythene bubble. In a few weeks roots will have established themselves in the moss, and it's time to snip the cutting clean from the mother plant and pot it in compost.

855 Free plants can be grown from pips and stones such as the avocado pear. Soak the stone in warm water and remove it from its outer covering. With its pointed end up, stick 3 tooth-picks into the sides of the stone so that it can now perch on the · rim of a wide-necked jar with its base in water. Keep the water level topped up. Pot when roots are developed.

856 Orange, lemon, tangerine and grapefruit provide indoor trees. Wash the pips and plant 3 or 4 to a small pot in sandy compost. In summer put them outside to make the wood harden.

857 For a pineapple plant, slice off the crown and plant the fleshy disc in a sand-based compost, or even in a saucer of water. They need lots of light and warmth – they'll die in less than 65°F (18°C).

Making Fresh Flowers Last

○ *Preservation and watering . . .*

858 So that flowers get the maximum amount of moisture up their stems without an airlock, cut off the bottom couple of inches (5 cm) under water.

859 For a colourful winter arrangement, bring in forsythia when it is in bud and watch the yellow flowers come out.

860 Add a foxglove or two to any cut flower decoration and they'll prolong the life of their companions considerably.

861 Heathers will last for weeks without their flowers wilting or needles dropping if kept without water. Stick the cut stems into a raw potato.

862 Stocks are anti-social and drink copious amounts. Keep them on their own in a large container and top up the water frequently.

863 Carnations are also best kept by themselves, but are one of the longest lasting of flowers if the stems are cut between 2 nodes – (nobbly bits on the stem) under water and left to have a drink for an hour or so in a bucketful of water before arranging. Bashing the stems accelerates their intake of water.

864 Flowers from spring bulbs are the only ones which don't need frequent changes of water. Cut them well above the white part of the stem and rinse the white residue under the tap. Giving them a generous pinch of salt will keep the water fresh and revive them when they look like flagging. Don't put daffodils and tulips in the same container.

| 865 | Tulips should first be wrapped securely in wet newspaper up to their heads and soaked in deep water to absorb the maximum amount and stop their heavy heads bending the stems. When arranging, a pin pushed just below the head on each stem will give them extra support. |

| 866 | Toss copper pennies in the water to keep tulips from drooping. |

| 867 | If taking roses from the garden, always cut to an outside leaf bud. Remove the lower leaves, strip the thorns and remove any damaged outer petals. Bash the base of the stems with a hammer to let in water. |

| 868 | All wood-stemmed flowers should have their ends crushed or split, as with roses. If they are showing signs of wilting, stand them for a short time in hot water. |

| 869 | Adding sugar to the water for chrysanthemums will keep them fresher longer. |

| 870 | Lessen the strong odour from cut marigolds by adding a teaspoon of sugar to the water. |

| 871 | Always strip the bottom leaves from cut flowers before placing them in a container. Leaves below the water level make the water slimy and smelly. |

| 872 | A teaspoon of household bleach added to the water of cut flowers prevents the water becoming cloudy, but the way to remove a slimy film from a stained vase is with bicarbonate of soda. |

| 873 | Short-stemmed flowers will keep fresh for double their life if placed in a bowl of well-watered sand. |

| 874 | Cut lily stems at a slant and put them in a bucket up to their necks in water before arranging. |

| 875 | Preserve a special single bloom indefinitely in a jar or bottle filled with surgical spirit. |

876 Singe the bottom of poppy stems with a candle or cigarette lighter before arranging.

877 Spraying cut flowers with a fine spray, especially where the atmosphere is dry with central heating or stale from smoke, keeps their faces cool and lets them take moisture through the leaves.

878 Nasturtiums shouldn't be added to arrangements, as they will kill off any flowers sharing a drink with them.

879 As with fish, Mondays should be given a miss when buying cut flowers – they will have been left over from the weekend.

880 Clean dust from dried flowers with a hairdryer.

○ *Revival techniques . . .*

881 A teaspoon of household detergent added to a quart (1.1 litres) of tepid water will revive most jaded cut flowers. So will lemonade, which is particularly appreciated by roses.

|882| After a few days a flower arrangement needs an overhaul. Cut back the stem ends and stand for a few seconds only in boiling water. Follow this with a cold drink for several hours immersed to the neck, prop them with newspapers if needs be before re-arranging.

|883| An aspirin in the water is the cure for many jaded flowers, but as with humans, it shouldn't be taken until needed.

○ *Novel ideas . . .*

|884| Tulips can be turned into dazzling oriental creations by gently turning the petals back to form an outward curve and reveal the stamens.

|885| If you're sending flowers abroad, place your order at least 2 weeks in advance if possible. Then the order goes by air mail letter, saving expensive telex and telephone charges.

|886| Keep a store of odd-shaped branches in large cardboard boxes, they will provide an eye-catching design with just the addition of a few flowers.

|887| A single orchid makes a perfect table decoration and they are not as expensive as is commonly believed. Kept in fresh water and cool conditions, a cut orchid will last for up to 6 weeks.

|888| Some of the easiest flowers and grasses to dry are achillea, African marigolds, larkspur, cow parsley, and delphiniums and physalis (Chinese lanterns). Essential to pick when just open. Hang upside down in bunches in a cool, dark place such as a pantry or cellar.

889 An assortment of leaves and bracken placed between sheets of newspaper under much trodden rugs, will be pressed dry for beautiful arrangements of autumn colours when the garden is bare.

890 Coat berries with nail varnish to stop them drying out or dropping. Spray unusually shaped foliage, seed pods and grasses with pewter or bronze paint from art shops for professional looking arrangements.

891 Wash and bleach magnolia leaves, attach them to wires and use in arrangements.

892 If your garden foliage is limited, treat selected leaves with 1 part glycerine to 2 of water and place in sunlight for a lighter colour.

Barbecues

893 Build your own with bricks, arranged in a hexagonal shape for best support, an old metal door scraper and the roasting pan from a domestic cooker.

894 A biscuit tin with the metal grid from a grill pan on top are easily portable for picnics and do the same job as shop-bought barbecues.

895 Whatever you use as a container for charcoal, line it first with aluminium foil, shiny side up and add a layer of gravel or sand. Makes it easier to clean afterwards and reflects the heat back on the food, speeding up the cooking process.

896 Never use volatile fuels such as petrol or paraffin to ignite the charcoal. They may be cheaper than purpose-made barbecue fuels, but they are dangerous and the fumes will ruin the taste of the food. White block firelighters or methylated spirits – used with care – are cheapest, but should always be allowed to burn out before putting food near them.

897 | Don't throw out packets or jars of dried herbs which are too old to add much flavour to food. Sprinkle some on the charcoal towards the end of cooking for an aroma to make your mouth water.

898 | The quickest way to clean off encrusted dirt from the grill is with mayonnaise applied on a wad of paper towels.

899 | A canister of baby wipes speedily mops up hands and utensils.

The Family Pet

Health
and Hygiene

900   A cat which simply refuses to take pills whole can be fed them powdered. Crush the tablets between the bowls of 2 teaspoons and add to a lump of butter. Spread this medicinal compound on the cat where he can lick it off.

901   With a dog, try pushing the pill into a soft-centered chocolate.

HE'LL ONLY EAT THE HARD ONES

902 Make a cheap anti-flea dog shampoo by mixing 1 part Dettol or TCP with 2 parts washing-up liquid and 3 parts water. Bottled, it will store indefinitely. Put a tablespoon of vinegar in the final rinse after every bath.

903 Use bicarbonate of soda as a dry shampoo and dog deodorant in winter.

904 For bad breath, rub bicarbonate of soda on a damp cloth over the animal's teeth.

905 Clean grease and stubborn dirt off fur, feathers and paws with Swarfega hand cleanser.

906 A chamois leather wrung out in a vinegar and warm water solution will remove the last stray hairs, deodorise the coat and act as a flea repellant between baths and after grooming sessions.

907 Take a tip from top cat and smooth-haired dog breeders and wipe over fur with a warm silk scarf for a coat like glass.

908 Keep old corduroy velvet to cut up as rags to dry off and polish up rain-soaked pets.

909 Puppy puddles call for immediate action with a squirt from a soda syphon. Rub over with some vinegar or ammonia on a cloth to remove the smell.

910 The smell and taste of oil of cloves deters puppies and kittens from chewing.

911 Stale bread, crisped and browned in the oven, makes into tasty rusks for adding to a dog's dinner.

912 A rubber ball floating on top of water stops it freezing. This can be useful for horse troughs.

913 A cold or chilled hamster goes to sleep and is apparently dead. Try a gentle warming with a hairdryer, or wrap in a woolly sock for a few hours in the airing cupboard . . .

914 A terrified hamster goes rigid and collapses, but can recover within a few days – don't be in too much of a hurry to bury him.

Comfort

915 A sheet of polystyrene provides good insulation in the dog or cat basket, but a newspaper lining also stops draughts and keeps in heat.

916 Keep a young puppy from fretting when removed from a litter, by putting a ticking clock and a hot-water bottle in his basket under a thick blanket.

917 Crisp dry leaves in autumn or gardener's peat make good bottom layers of bedding for rabbits and guinea pigs, but never make hay from grass cuttings or feed them fresh cuttings if they may have been contaminated by lawn mower oil.

918 When a pond freezes over in winter, melt the ice by sitting a hot kettle on top. Smashing it sends shock waves through the water which can kill pond fish.

919 | Keep or collect small children's woollens at jumble sales. These provide pullovers for old, sick and arthriticky animals when heating goes off at night. Polo neck jerseys with the arms rolled up are particularly good . . .

Household Pests

920 | Flies hate mint, basil or nettles. The country custom is to hang up bunches in doorways or open windows.

921 | Hair spray keeps flies' wings in place and stops them flying around, fast.

922 | It is said that ants never cross a chalk line. They also dislike mint, cloves and turpentine, and you can trap them with a bait of borax mixed with sugar. Where there are animals and children, pouring boiling water on an ants' nest is safer.

923 | Mice also are allergic to mint. Put a few drops of essence of peppermint on cottonwool and leave near mouseholes. Alternatively, keep bunches of watercress near mouse-tempting food in a pantry.

924 | Wasps – make a trap using a screw-top jar containing sugar, jam or honey in a little warm water. Pierce a few holes in the top with a beer can opener, leaving holes big enough for wasps to get in, but small enough to make their escape impossible.

○ *Moths . . .*

925 Always wash any new piece of furniture which comes into your home in a strong ammonia and water solution to fumigate. Moths are allergic to lavender, cloves, oranges, and cedarwood furniture.

926 Kill off moth eggs in a carpet by using a hot iron over a damp cloth and pressing until bone dry.

Kids' Stuff

Emergencies

927 Problems tend to occur when you are already late for school. Have handy a panic box with loose change, buttons, already-threaded and knotted needles with black and white cotton, a single cheque and pen, shoe laces, safety pin and sellotape. Replace as soon as anything is used up.

928 Toothpaste applied to a bee sting gives instant relief.

929 Get chewing gum off clothing by first scraping off as much as possible and tackling the residue with white spirit. Pointless to wash it.

930 Chewing gum on hair can be gently coaxed off with baby oil on a cotton wool pad.

Child-Care

931 You can make considerable savings by ordering nappies in bulk from local suppliers. Ask at your baby clinic, and perhaps get together with other mothers to pay for a delivery between you.

932 Start a babysitting pool in your area, exchanging points rather than money. After midnight can count as 2 points an hour towards your credit rating.

933 If electric light switches in a child's room are painted with phosphorescent paint, they needn't worry about getting up in the dark.

○ *Bath-time . . .*

934 To prevent or remove scurf on babies' heads before bathing, rub on a little petroleum jelly.

935 If you don't have a mat for the bottom of the bath, improvise by spreading a towel on the bottom for a non-slip surface.

936 A squirt of washing-up liquid in the bath before adding dirty children will prevent a scum line forming and will make it easier to clean afterwards.

937   For tiny tots, bathing them in a plastic laundry basket inside the big bath gives extra security.

Clothes

938   For extra security, where a child's jacket has an inside pocket sew a small zip.

939   If your two children have different initials, order one lot of name tabs with both initials at different sides of the surname. Just bend one end under as appropriate when sewing on.

940   To make a child's painting smock, take an old shirt, shorten the sleeves and put elastic round the cuffs. Remove the tails and when worn back to front, the tailpieces can make a front pocket.

941   Knees and elbows of children's clothes wear out quickest, but sew-on patches which stick out a mile are generally unpopular. Patches sewn or stuck on the inside to protect the material do almost as well.

942   Two inch (5 cm) cotton bandaging is the stuff to use for making false hems when good clothes are outgrown.

○   *Shoes . . .*

943   Sandpaper the soles of new boots and shoes to prevent slipping whilst they are being worn in.

944   If you rub a wet cloth over a childs' shoe laces before tying them, they'll tighten and be less likely to come undone when dry.

Play-Time

945 | Use large rolls of kitchen foil for a practical tablecloth at a children's party.

946 | Plastic trays from chocolate boxes are good for novely shaped ice cubes for children's party drinks.

947 | Make ice lollies for next to nothing. Pour fruit juice (slightly diluted squash), chocolate or strawberry milk-shakes into ice trays. Put a cocktail stick in each one before they set.

948 | For an economical anytime snack which all children seem to love, dip slices of bread in beaten egg to which a little milk has been added, fry lightly on both sides until golden brown, and serve hot with a sweet or savoury spread or a sprinkling of cinammon.

949 | Keep a list of free entertainment. Ask your local Tourist Authority what's on, or consult the local papers. Make use of libraries for books and records and ring theatres for midweek bargains.

950 | Fillings for soft toys are more expensive than they need be. Save old woollen jumpers or buy them at jumble sales, wash and dry them well, unravel the wool and chop it up into a springy filling. Chopped up tights can also be added.

951 | Small pots of paint are very expensive; you pay a lot for the packaging. Shop around for big squeezy bottles of vivid coloured, ready-mixed water-based paints.

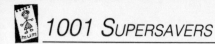

952   A roll of cheap wall-lining paper from decorator's shops, cut into big sheets and pinned to a board, will delight any child who likes to paint or draw.

953   If bottles of paper glue become hardened, add a little vinegar to soften.

954   Make a budget modelling dough with 3 cups of flour, 1 cup of salt and 1 cup of water plus any food colouring. By the time it's kneaded well it's ready for use, and will keep for a day or so in a sealed plastic bag.

On the Move

955 If your bank knows you as a regular customer, they should be happy to take a box with jewellery and other valuables on safe deposit and free of charge, whilst you are on holiday. Do check, however, as you order your travellers' cheques.

956 Save time by being organised. A 'going away' list can be used every year with just a little updating. Helps fill insurance forms if you can refer to a list of contents in stolen luggage.

957 One of the cheapest ways to have a family holiday is house swapping. Takes care of what to do with pets, plants etc.

958 If you intend to complain about some aspect of your holiday, take photographs where appropriate or exchange addresses with others who shared your views. Keep bills for extra expenses incurred by bad service and note the names of any staff members involved.

959 If you get a flat tyre on a car journey and can't get the jack underneath, drive onto the spare tyre to lift the car up.

960 When leaving the house for long periods, leave a blanket on top of beds to prevent damp. The bed will still be dry after 2 or 3 weeks, but the blanket will then need airing.

Luggage and Packing

961 Use that Christmas present of scented drawer liners in between layers of clothing to ensure a scented crease-free wardrobe at the other end.

962 Clothes folded around rolled up plastic bags will resist creases better in packing.

963 Always fold across a garment rather than lengthways, so that the weight when it's hung up will help remove the creases faster.

964 A strap around a suitcase, after you've locked it, not only gives better protection but gives airport thieves less of a chance to open it quickly.

965 If your travelling bag is a popular make, give it a distinguishing stick-on label. It's easy to take an identical one from a carousel and not realise the mistake until you're at your hotel.

966 Invest in a suitcase with wheels, or buy a clip-on set to save time and the energy wasted lugging a heavy suitcase around.

967 | Putting your name and work address or bank, rather than details of your home on labels, means that it's less likely to be broken into in your absence.

968 | Buy hats, small carry bags and some of your clothes when you get there. They will most likely be cheaper . . .

969 | Keep an old spectacle case in your hand luggage with useful travel bits – aspirins, needles and cotton, safety pins, sticking plaster, nail scissors, the front-door key . . .

970 | Dental floss doubles up as string and as an emergency sewing thread if buttons or zips on clothes and luggage give way.

Health
and Comfort

971 | Travel sickness can often be allayed by chewing glucose tablets, which double as an energy boost on a long journey.

972 | You can buy inflatable head pillows which have endless uses – when flights are delayed, you want a nap on the beach etc. Well worth the money.

973 | Oil of cloves is the traveller's favourite for treating toothache, but a pad of cotton wool soaked in whisky or gin takes away the pain in an emergency.

974 | Citronella is an old-fashioned mosquito repellent. One inexpensive small bottle from the chemist should last a fortnight. It also soothes bites.

975 | Repellents last longer on clothes and sheets than on your skin, where the perspiration can wash it off quite quickly.

976 | Before you go on a walking holiday, pre-condition the feet for at least a week before by rubbing night and morning with surgical spirit.

Transport

977 In some countries, where labour is comparatively cheap, it's often scarcely more expensive to hire a car complete with driver than to hire one without. That way you'll probably get a more reliable car!

978 Coach travel is cheaper than rail and often far more comfortable. Ask your travel agent, local bus company and railway station about special offers.

○ *Air travel . . .*

979 It pays to check in really early for international flights. They can be as much as 25 per cent overbooked. Your ticket does not guarantee a seat on a particular flight.

980 Most airlines are happy to provide games, colouring materials and other more essential items for children such as baby food, nappies and cots. Cut down on hand luggage, and don't be afraid to ask.

| 981 | Airlines most likely won't mind if you take a couple of their stout sick-bags as a memento of your journey. Useful for those mountainous hair-pin bends when travelling by car with children later in the holiday. |

| 982 | If a child requires a special diet, or vegetarian, let your booking agent know in advance to order it. |

| 983 | Buy your duty-free goods in airport lounges where they are generally cheaper than on the plane and the choice is greater. |

| 984 | If you are travelling independently, it may be cheaper to buy your return tickets abroad. |

Kids and Pets

| 985 | Buttering a cat's paws stops it from straying when moved to a new home, but provide a litter tray and keep your pet in for a couple of days as an extra precaution. |

| 986 | Moving house can be traumatic for small children. Give each child a dustbin liner with his own personal things in it, labelled with his name. That night he can unpack sleeping bag, night things, a favourite toy and book, plus fresh clothes for the morning. |

987 Even more upsetting than going to an unknown territory, is the actual removal itself. It's better to board pets out, away from the tension and clatter of a removal, and then collect once you're installed in the home. The same can apply to children.

988 Postage stamps which are stuck together will separate easily if popped into the fridge for a few minutes.

989 Rubbing candle wax from the bottom of a candle over ink on a parcel after you've written it protects it from rain.

990 Rub lighter fuel on the inside of an envelope behind the stamp to remove it – it's safer and quicker than steaming.

991 Don't buy car polishes – a bucket of hot water with a cupful of paraffin added will give a protective shine if allowed to dry in its own time.

992 Brasso will often remove scratches on car paint.

993 To wash dirty hands after working on the car, rub washing-up liquid undiluted into the hands and let it dry on the skin for a couple of minutes before washing off in the usual way.

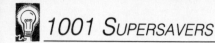

| 994 | To prevent frozen car locks, cover them over with sticky tape. |

| 995 | It's much cheaper to buy rolls of sticky address labels and recycle envelopes from junk mail than to buy new envelopes to send off bills etc. |

| 996 | Aerosol cans often clog up when only half empty. Remove the nozzle and place it in boiling water for a minute or so. |

| 997 | Nozzles of aerosol paint cans, soaked in paraffin or paint stripper overnight should function again. |

| 998 | Spectacles given an occasional rub with methylated spirit will come up sparkling clean. |

| 999 | Before throwing out apparently dried-up ball-point pens, pop them in a bowl of hot water or run under the tap for a couple of minutes. The chances are they'll write again. |

| 1000 | When batteries are on their last legs try warming them – they'll last just that little bit longer. |

| 1001 | Bicycle tyres when not in use need a wipe over with a damp cloth to stop them cracking. |